Your

of related interest

ADHD—Living without Brakes
Martin L. Kutscher MD
Illustrated by Douglas Puder, MD
ISBN 978 1 84310 873 3 HARDBACK
ISBN 978 1 84905 816 2 PAPERBACK

The ADHD Handbook
A Guide for Parents and Professionals
Alison Munden and Jon Arcelus
ISBN 978 1 85302 756 7

Parenting the ADD Child
Can't Do? Won't Do? Practical Strategies for Managing
Behaviour Problems in Children with ADD and ADHD
David Pentecost
ISBN 978 1 85302 811 3

Understanding Motor Skills in Children with Dyspraxia,
ADHD, Autism, and Other Learning Disabilities
A Guide to Improving Coordination
Lisa A. Kurtz
Part of the JKP Essentials series
ISBN 978 1 84310 865 8

Organize
Your ADD/ADHD
Child

A Practical Guide for Parents

CHERYL R. CARTER

Jessica Kingsley *Publishers*
London and Philadelphia

First published in 2011
by Jessica Kingsley Publishers
116 Pentonville Road
London N1 9JB, UK
and
400 Market Street, Suite 400
Philadelphia, PA 19106, USA

www.jkp.com

Library of Congress Cataloging in Publication Data
A CIP catalog record for this book is available from the Library of Congress

British Library Cataloguing in Publication Data
A CIP catalogue record for this book is available from the British Library

ISBN 978 1 84905 839 1

Printed and bound in the United States by
Thomson-Shore, 7300 Joy Road, Dexter, MI 48130

Dedicated to my students

DISCLAIMER

This book is not intended to diagnose, treat or evaluate Attention Deficit Disorder or Attention Deficit Disorder with Hyperactivity (ADD/ADHD). The author and publisher assume an accurate diagnosis has been made clinically or educationally and the reader is acting on that information. See the list of organizations in the useful resources section for information and resources on ADD/ADHD issues. Please be aware that this book will solely address the issues of disorganization and time management in relation to ADD/ADHD itself.

The author recognizes that the term ADHD is the correct medical term and that there are primarily three variations of ADHD: inattentive, hyperactive-impulsive and combined. Most parents refer to ADHD as ADD and therefore this book generally refers to ADD to be representative of all the medical forms of ADHD. See the list of useful resources at the end of the text for information on ADD/ADHD.

Please note that when referring to the child with ADD, he/she and his/her are used interchangeably throughout this book.

Contents

Introduction: No More Lost Homework

LET'S BEGIN

Missing homework again? You saw him do it and told him to put it in his backpack, so where could it be? This is not the first time. You've tried everything—threats, taking away privileges, giving privileges, but nothing seems to work. You have heard that ADD children are difficult to organize but it just cannot go on any longer. You need help. Traditional methods just don't seem to work with your child. Children with ADD generally have difficulty focusing or concentrating on a task. Additionally, these children are also known for being impulsive, highly distractible, indecisive, forgetful and chronically disorganized.

ADD is much more complex than just the symptoms but the scope of this book is to address those typical ADD disorganization symptoms. The term ADD will generally be used but the ideas equally apply to ADHD children. In my previous book *Clean Your Room So I Can At Least See the Floor*, I introduced the F.I.R.S.T. way to organize children. I have found most children can easily be organized if organization incorporates fun, values them as individuals, guides them with rules, keeps the whole process simple and teaches basic time management principles. Fun, individualism, rules, simplicity and time management are the keys to organizing children. Taking the first letter of each of the five elements (fun, individualism, rules, simplicity and time management) we get the acronym F.I.R.S.T. These elements are all based on an understanding of child development and human nature and can easily be applied to ADD children.

The premise of the F.I.R.S.T. way to organize is that we build on the F.I.R.S.T. model by adding a second layer for ADD children. These children need fun balanced with firmness, individuality with an emphasis on their interests, rules with a regular routine, simplicity coupled with specifics, and time management with an understanding of transitions. I will discuss each of these steps in detail as we progress through the book.

The F.I.R.S.T. method works well when we consciously apply it to our organizing efforts because it addresses core issues of child development. Nearly all children want to have fun, be recognized as an individual, require the safety of structure and rules, need to be communicated to on their level in a simple way so they can easily understand, and, finally, they need to develop time consciousness.

Before we can delve into the execution of the F.I.R.S.T. approach, let's lay a foundation on how children are trained. Training with children occurs in five sequential steps. Some ADD children may need to be prodded through the steps. For instance, ADD children may enjoy your company so much in step one that they are reluctant to master a skill and then move to the next step. You may have to insist the child move along even if she is resistant initially.

The following steps are generally the way children are trained to do household chores.

STEP ONE—DEMONSTRATE

This is the basic step. Simply allow your child to observe you several times doing a task. Toddlers and preschoolers do this naturally (notice how their play imitates what they see in real life). For instance, if you want your child to make his bed, let him observe you making your bed several times. Talk to him about the steps involved in making his bed as he watches you make the bed. This step has to be deliberate. You cannot just assume your child knows how to do a task if he has not intentionally observed you performing the task.

To maintain your child's attention during this step, have him actively imitate you. For example, he can pretend he is smoothing the wrinkles by panning his hands in the air pantomiming the motion while you are actually smoothing the wrinkles on the bed. It is essential that children are doing something other than just watching you. Many ADD children need to engage in motion to really concentrate on instruction. If you force an ADD child to be completely still he may be focused on staying still and miss out on everything you are saying to him. Older children may find it silly to pantomime but they can still illustrate with their hands or speak aloud each step necessary to complete the task successfully.

STEP TWO—PARTICIPATE

This next step is to let your child help you make his bed. Take note of his mistakes or weak points. Correct mistakes and address any weak areas. Do not rush through this step. He should assist you in a few bed-making sessions as he gradually assumes more responsibility for the task until he is practically doing the job himself.

Do not exasperate your child by expecting perfection. A job well done does not have to look exactly as if you had done it yourself but expect a reasonable proximity. You will want to spend sufficient time with your ADD child in this step but do not let your child rely too much on you. Encourage your child to make independent steps.

STEP THREE—SUPERVISE

The third step is to watch your child make his bed. If he still has difficulty making the bed (performing the task), do not jump in to help him. Instead, ask him what the next step is. At this step, you want to direct your child verbally. The supervision step is when you correct any errors and problems so this step cannot be rushed. Once you are assured your child has mastered this step, confidently move to the next step.

ADD children tend to need a lot of immediate positive feedback and clear direction. You may have to supervise ADD children a bit longer and closer because they need more assurance and positive feedback than other children.

STEP FOUR—DELEGATE

The fourth step after your child has mastered bed making (the task) is to delegate the task to your child. Delegation may mean the chore is placed on his chore chart or you may make a contract with an older child.

When placing the chore on the child's chore chart make a big deal about how he has matured into the task and can handle it independently. If possible, let the child conveniently overhear you talking to your partner, mother or a neighbor about how responsible the child is and that he just got a new chore assignment on his chart.

STEP FIVE—INSPECT

The fifth step almost seems unnecessary but occasionally you should inspect his bed. Be certain to give plenty of praise and affirmation for learning a new skill. Children do not do what we expect but only what we inspect.

ADD children really need to know you are going to inspect what they do. They inherently want to please you and really need your feedback. Do frequent spot inspections. This keeps your child on his toes while relieving you of the tedium of inspecting every day. Generally, you want your ADD children to know you will inspect their chores at least once a week because they need a firm deadline since messes do not bother them.

These five steps are fundamental to training your ADD child. Training your child may take time but in the end, your child will feel affirmed and enjoy contributing to the family.

KEY POINTS

- When it is necessary to repeat yourself to your child for clarity or reinforcement, say it in a different way. You can sometimes play the whisper game where you whisper loudly the instructions. Your child will focus in on a whisper.

- As much as possible attempt to give instructions in a quiet environment. Do not say "I already told you that" because most likely he did not hear you. Simply repeat it in your normal voice tone.

- After your child finishes one phase of a chore ask him to do as many jumping jacks as he can in two minutes. He needs movement and the movement also gets the brain engaged for him to concentrate on the next chore.

- Your child will do better with assigned chores that are short in duration so try to get his assigned chores down to a few minutes. You can add more chores as he perfects the shorter ones.

1 Make It Fun But Keep It Firm

The F.I.R.S.T. approach begins with making organization fun. Children, like us, gravitate to the pleasurable. Adding an element of fun motivates almost any child to do anything; in fact, the ingenious parent will couple every tedious task with a reward. Work is fun; it is all a matter of perception. Tom Sawyer tricked his friends into painting the fence just by changing their perceptions of the task. Fun will get children to move. While fun will motivate most children to move, ADD children also need firm boundaries. Because of their impulsivity they need to have their attention positively directed when having fun. They really need their fun balanced with firm boundaries.

Firmness does not mean harshness. Quite the contrary, it merely means that fun does not result in chaos. ADD children tend to become overly stimulated or experience extreme emotional arousal in social situations where there is little control. Even a friendly birthday party with minimal supervision can spell disaster for the impulsive ADD child. Aimless running around only exacerbates hyperactivity in some children. Physical activity with a purpose is best for ADD children. Fun must occur within firm guidelines.

Fun is beneficial for ADD children because it releases endorphins, which will help with a bad mood, anxiety and depression. These disorders are a common secondary diagnosis in ADD children. If we can couple fun with daily chores, we are aiding our children emotionally and helping them to be organized at the same time. ADD children also have a low tolerance for boring activities. Making their work fun ensures they are motivated to do their chores with a minimum number of reminders. Fun also helps them to develop good habits because habits are formed through repetition. We automatically repeat the pleasurable.

Clearly, fun balanced with firm boundaries serves the ADD child both short and long term. Anything can be made fun. You can start by using your child's imagination. A child's imagination can make almost any task fun. My eight year old once told me she likes putting items back in their places in our home by pretending she is running her own delivery service. A chore I would normally have to struggle with getting her to do, she willingly does when she can be a pretend delivery person.

Take advantage of your child's wild and vivid imagination but make sure you put some boundaries in place. Brainstorm with your child on possible home chores that can be transformed into an actual role. Pick a task, like mopping the floor, and ask what he imagines doing while mopping. He might say painting a mural or cleaning an elephant. Run with the idea. Be careful not to criticize your child's imaginative ideas. What sounds silly to you may really motivate your child. Be silly with your child and write on his chore chart "clean the elephant." You might even say "I see a spot on the elephant's tail" if your child forgets to mop a portion of the floor. This keeps the chores fun and light.

Fun is the key word here. Sit down and brainstorm on ways to make jobs fun. You may be surprised at your child's imagination especially if you prime the pump with suggestions like being a family delivery person. To prevent your child impulsively changing from an agreed-upon role to another, get items of clothing to reinforce the role/task. For instance, if you want your child to clean up after himself, and perhaps other family members, get him an old hat so he can be a delivery person. You can find almost any item at a thrift store or online auction website. If you are prone to a bit of distraction yourself write on a sticky or post-it note that you are going online to find an old delivery person's cap and give yourself a designated time to find one. If this would take too long simply make a hat out of construction paper or paste the words 'delivery person' on an old cap.

Follow children around the house or at least check their bags/sacks when you first assign this job to them. Be clear that they are only to pick up items that are out of place. Those items can be placed in a family lost and found box for family members to retrieve on their own. In our family, we charge money to get items out of the lost and found box.

Any chore can be made into a game by using a timer. Timers can be used by children to race against time itself when completing a chore. Set the timer and let the child play beat the clock/timer. Brothers and sisters should not be timed against one another because the competition fosters sibling rivalry. I prefer to use a digital timer with a large screen on which children can actually see the numbers escalating or descending, although when working with children with ADD an analog timer (one on which the child can see time passing) works best. See my list of useful resources at the end of this book. Visually being able to see the passage of time helps the child pace himself. The clicking of the seconds also keeps the child aware that time is really passing. It fosters time awareness.

ADD children hate anything that is boring, so keep them moving. Engage them in perpetual movement. Preschoolers like to sing as they put away their toys. You can make up clean-up songs to popular tunes like "Row, row, row your boat" and change the lyrics to "Pick, pick up your toys." The movement and music will reinforce the activity and the process. Older children will enjoy cleaning to their favorite music. You might also make a game by seeing how many songs your child can play on her MP3 player before her bedroom is clean. Older children may dance around while they clean their rooms. Be firm here; movement should be purposeful and not aimless.

Some parents are concerned that a chore will be done slipshod because children are using a timer or dancing around to music while cleaning. Your child should not be dancing or timed on tasks they have not mastered. The music or timer is utilized to remove the tediousness from the chore. Fully train your child to do a task before you utilize the timer or music. ADD children may need to work from a list especially when dancing and cleaning. The job should be done in excellence, not just quickly. If your child does a sloppy job, give him more time to complete a task and let him know neatness counts. If necessary, have him repeat a sloppy job until it is done correctly. The repetition is not to be punitive. A fun approach might be how quickly you can correct your mistakes. Another idea, which has worked with ADD children who are big picture thinkers, is to set the timer and see how slowly they can finish a chore. They will be forced to slow down and tend to the details of a task.

Nearly all chores can be made into a game. The "Chore Jar Game" is a favorite game for large families. Small families may overwhelm the ADD child with too many tasks. This game is great for children because it motivates them to do more household chores. It also occupies the ADD child in a positive activity. To play the game, first, write down the chores for the week on index cards and assign the chores points based on how difficult or tedious the task may be for children. For instance, loading the dishwasher carries more points than feeding the goldfish. Once a week your children would draw cards to see which chores they would do. To encourage camaraderie and good will among siblings allow children to earn extra points by helping a younger sibling with difficult or tedious chores. The winner, the child with the most points at the end of the week, gets a prize.

You will need to establish firm boundaries with your ADD child to make sure he does not snatch cards from siblings. He may have points deducted from his final score if he pushes his siblings instead of waiting his turn to draw his cards. ADD children also tend to have a low frustration threshold. The frustration tolerance can only be built by incrementally increasing the time your child has to wait. If possible, give your child something harmless to fidget with while he waits. Pipe cleaners, small snuggly toys, or plastic hand exercisers are good to distract children while they are waiting and anticipating a turn.

Praise your child immensely for waiting. You might even point out to your child how many minutes she has waited and reward her with a hug or praise. It is not a good idea to give our children tangible prizes each time they achieve a goal because it fosters a performance mentality in them. You might also ask your child after she has been able to wait her turn if she feels good about herself. Comment how patient she is because she is now able to wait her turn a whole two minutes. This helps her visualize herself as successful. In addition, identifying the exact time she has waited will encourage her gradually to increase her waiting time or frustration threshold. She will view herself as successful.

Self-perception goes a long way in children. If a child sees herself as successful, she will set herself up for success. We become what we think we are. Perception is a powerful motivator. When we speak positively to ourselves generally, we get positive results. Negative talk is best corrected in a non-threatening atmosphere. It is best to correct your child's negative talk when you are doing something fun. The child feels less intimidated and is more likely to listen to you. So keep the fun going. Listen to the reason your child may object to doing a task. If dusting is a chore your child does not like, substitute the old dust rag for a feather duster. What kid can resist feathers? Simple substitutions work wonders.

Remember always to be specific about what needs to be done for the room to be clean or orderly. We will discuss later the need for children to know specifically what is expected of them. You must be firm in your expectations. Promise a reward immediately for a task completed. You may also make your child the official Clean-up Family person. Ask him to report to you after he has made sure everyone has done their chores. He must also assist everyone since he is the leader. It is a great opportunity to teach your child about servant leadership and build his social skills. A good leader is always willing to do what he wants his followers to do. It also puts your child in the favored position of a leader, a position ADD children typically do not often hold.

Fun should never overshadow the job being done. But as a parent, do not assume that some things just have to be done without it being fun. Even waking up in the morning can be fun. See the list of useful resources for flying and rolling alarm clocks. Hot pancakes can motivate even the most procrastinating child to get up in the morning. Of course, you have to be firm that the child has to come to the breakfast table in an allotted amount of time to enjoy the pancakes. If you are not firm the fun factor will backfire on you because you will reinforce your child's bad habits.

Even tedious tasks can be made into fun activities if everyone does them together. Invite your child to do chores with you. Be silly and engage the child in conversation. There are so many ways you can tie fun to everyday activities. Play Simon Says when it's time for your child to clean up. Give one command at a time or else you will overwhelm your ADD child. She can only pay attention to one instruction at a time. If you are in doubt as to how to make something fun simply offer a reward when the job is complete. Large seasonal jobs like cleaning the garage or lawn work should be rewarded incrementally with the biggest reward arriving only after the job is completed.

Fun is a powerful motivator and when balanced with firmness can really get your ADD child to embrace work and develop new habits. Besides getting your child to do household chores the fun factor can also be used to help the child develop good sanitary habits. A basic morning hygiene checklist with such things as face washing and teeth brushing can be coupled with a reward. You can also use a timer to get your child to focus on the task.

Fun with boundaries or firmness is one primary way you will get results. It is almost so simple that many parents overlook the potential. The next step reinforces the importance of valuing the individuality of your child.

FURTHER TIPS

- Make a lost and found box for items not put in their proper place. Make kids pay or do extra chores to get items out of the box. Family members should only be allowed to retrieve misplaced items from the box during scheduled times during the week so you are not constantly inconvenienced.

- When a television commercial comes on, do a household task and see who can be the first one back on the couch and back to the show before everyone else. You can also use a timer and everyone can run and see what chore they can do the fastest.

- Hide money around a room and tell your child if he thoroughly cleans the room he should have a dollar in coins (or whatever amount you determine). He will clean thoroughly looking for the money.

- Allow your younger children to use imaginative play. For instance, your daughter can be the delivery person returning misplaced items to their correct spots. You can even make this a daily family chore for a toddler or preschooler who likes to pretend.

2 Individualize With Interests

The second step of the F.I.R.S.T. approach is to individualize the organization process for our children. Our children want to be validated as individuals. From birth our children are moving toward independence and we can capitalize on this fact by gracing them with the freedom to be their own individuals. Even the stoic toddler who grimaces no to our every request is really just expressing independence. Children like to express their personality and this can become a valuable organizing incentive for us.

They want to be unique and as long as we help them to stand out from the crowd, they will embrace our organizing efforts. ADD children are no exception. Sometimes parents and professionals get so clinical with children with ADD challenges that we tend to forget they are individuals with their own interests and ideas.

Our children need to know that they are individuals and that their interests and ideas matter to us. Often parents get so caught up in managing ADD behavior that they forget to look at each child individually. I have been guilty of this on many occasions. I can get so caught up in managing behavior that I forget to embrace the individual who is still going to make mistakes, have temper tantrums, lose things, forget assignments, etc., in spite of my best efforts.

ADD children are very creative and if we accept them as individuals and embrace their interests and ideas, we can save ourselves a lot of time and effort. For instance, if your child likes dinosaurs, get dinosaur notebooks, pencils, etc. He is less likely to lose items he feels are important to him. This will not guarantee that he will never lose another pencil but it does provide incentive for him.

What are your child's interests? You can begin in your child's room. It should reflect your child's personality and interests. Children often like celebrities, sports figures and cartoon characters. Purchase bedding and room accessories that reflect their likes and aspirations. The child will have a real investment in the room and want to keep it clean. A room makeover guarantees enthusiasm and cooperation. Capitalize on your child's desire for a room makeover and seize the opportunity to purge her clutter and to strategize a way to maintain a clean room. By offering to do a room makeover as opposed to just cleaning your child's room for her, you communicate to the child that you care about her interests and you are not just concerned about the messiness of the room and how it reflects on you and your home. A room makeover keeps the focus on the child and her interests.

The reality is that even after the makeover your ADD child will have trouble maintaining an orderly room. Keeping a room organized can be overwhelming so be prepared to offer to help. He will need systems to maintain his room. Remember your child is not purposefully trying to drive you insane by having his room look like the county dump. He genuinely needs organizing systems to help him. ADD children actually think better in organized environments so it is important that the living quarters are neat. It all starts with you organizing the room for them.

Organize the room around different purposes or zones. Typical children's bedroom zones might include reading, studying, music, craft and play. Rotate toys, monthly or quarterly, by storing some temporarily in the closet on a top shelf (in a plastic storage container) out of reach of the child. This serves two purposes: the child is not overwhelmed with too many toys and the room will stay neater when the child has access to fewer toys. Older children can store their prized possessions on the closet shelves.

Be creative. Use clear shoeboxes or storage bins so that you can easily identify the contents. You can also make use of the wall space by installing shelves or a poster border. Under the bed storage containers are a great way to store toys children usually play with in the room. When you are helping your child to be organized, the room and storage must reflect the child too. Keep the child's interests in mind. Choose low storage for children who are crawlers and high storage like shelves for children who prefer to display their items. After you have put your child's room in order, younger children may need a weekly and/or daily room maintenance checklist to keep their room orderly. Older children will require a contract.

Contracts demonstrate to our children that we trust and respect them as individuals. While chore charts may work for little ones, contracts work best on chores such as cleaning a room that have the potential to spark family conflict. Conflicts are dissipated when all the parties involved have a general understanding of one another's expectations. A good contract is one drawn up by you and your child together with both of you making some concessions. I once drew up a contract for my son on what we collectively agreed a clean room meant. Thus, when I asked him to clean his room we had a viable checklist that we derived from the contract that he could work from to clean the room.

Contracts should not be used to impose our standards and ideas on our children. This will only breed resistance because the child will feel forced into your mold and robbed of their individuality. A child's sense of self is in part derived from the way those who love him interact with him. Each child wants to know their opinions, interests and desires are valued. Young children have difficulty separating what they like from who they are; therefore, we should never criticize our children's interests. We need to value our children in word and deed. This is precisely why making contracts works with children because it shows you value them as persons and that you are not heaping unfair and unwarranted punishment on them.

Contracts also work because they remove us from the role of enforcer. The child is responsible for keeping her word. Arguments diminish because a child cannot argue with a piece of paper. Contracts work well when children draw them up with you because they do not feel like rules are imposed on them. Older ADD children who recognize their inherent weakness may actually embrace a contract because it helps them to be more decisive. A contract can be made for just about any parenting dilemma. This keeps the impulsive child from making a decision on the spot if he is aware of his contract. Naturally, ADD children will have a greater challenge remembering the contract details so keep the wording simple and direct.

ADD children need help remembering. The trick is to remind them without babying or belittling them and embracing their individuality and interests. You can easily remind an older child about a contract rather than a behavior. For instance, instead of nagging your child to pick up his room you might just point out that it is time to review the contract. This puts the responsibility on the child to review the contract and perhaps pick up the papers in his room, etc., as it is reflected in the contract. A contract is a neutral piece of paper and it generally seems fair to the child. Contracts also have the added benefit of keeping parent/child relationships healthy because a parent is not constantly reprimanding the child. Contracts are perceived to be fair because children do not feel forced to do something.

Nearly all children have an ingrained sense of fairness. Therefore, housework forced upon them is seen as drudgery.

Housework and chores must be seen as an honor or a privilege. It is a matter of perception. All chores should be viewed honorably. When a child is old enough, both physically and cognitively, and adequately trained, she may be able to mow the lawn. Celebrate the occasion; pull out the camcorder to capture her first time mowing the lawn. Making a big deal of chores can turn them into rites of passage into adulthood, really indicating to the child that the job is a valuable grown-up task.

Most children want to be grown up so if doing the dishes is viewed as an adult's task then they will want to do the dishes. You will have to be careful not to say you dread doing the dishes and want to pass it off if you want the task to be embraced as a privilege. The tasks have to be seen as honorable. "Honorable tasks are given to honorable and dependable people" is the message you want to give your child. Until they are capable of doing the dishes you may have to show enthusiasm for doing dishes yourself. I realize it is hard but in the process you are also teaching your child to have a good attitude and you might actually begin to enjoy doing the dishes.

You do not gain a good attitude to manipulate your child into chore compliance. Your positive attitude will liberate you from a negative disposition. Many parents confess they feel abused and put upon by their families simply because they wrestle with thoughts of just being a glorified slave for their families. If you have these thoughts and unconsciously pass them on to your children then your children will feel abused and devalued just like you. This will negatively affect your relationship with your children because they will not feel validated by you. Chores should help actualize your child positively as he contributes to the family. Begin to see your role and household tasks as sacred and your child will follow your lead. As you feel validated and strength in your own individuality you will free your child to embrace the same positive attitudes.

ADD children need consistent reminders. Different colors can be used for your child's possessions. This works if you have a big family and the child realizes the red towel, cup, toothbrush, etc., all belong to him. This has the added benefit of knowing who left the wet towel on the floor. The color choice should be made by your child. Personal choices work because the child has an emotional investment in keeping up with his items. Emotional or personal investment goes a long way with ADD children. ADD children can be resistant and we need to gain their compliance as much as possible.

Imposing one's way of doing something is the surest way to get resistance from our children. Some ADD children are naturally resistant so it is imperative we help them to feel a part of our team and valued as human beings. Our children did not come to us in tidy little packages to be assembled according to directions. No, the beauty and richness of the relationship with our children is that we must keep trying several different things until we chance upon one that works for our family.

Sometimes we also need to use different methods for siblings. The point is that we just have to keep trying but that is part of what being a parent is all about: never giving up, and seeing our children as individuals and not a prognosis. Just taking an objective look at your child will help you determine which organizing strategies will or won't work with him. We cannot become so clinical with our children that we lose sight of their interests and individuality. Even the fun activities we choose must reflect our children's individuality. Individuality and fun must also be balanced with rules. We will look at this next.

FURTHER TIPS

- Offer to be your child's servant and help him complete chores so he knows you are on his team. Surprise your child and make his bed or do a chore for him. It will show him you really care and motivate him to do his chores more out of a relationship than a regiment.

- Allow each family member to post their schedule on the family calendar as per their designated colors (red, black, blue, green ink). Everyone should have their own organizing space. Give your child his or her own desk. Encourage your child to schedule her own daily quiet time. Put planning time into the family's weekly schedule. Post family schedules throughout the house as a reminder.

- Provide your child with tools to help her be successful. Get your child a pocket file folder for school correspondence. Insert your child's favorite music cassette in her cassette/alarm clock. It is a pleasant way to wake up.

- Look your child in the eye and give verbal and physical (i.e. hugs) praise and affirmation when your child has completed a task. Children naturally seek our approval and acceptance.

3 Establish Rules With a Routine

Rules balance the other two schemas of fun and individuality. A child who has fun all the time and always expresses his individuality will be reckless. Children need rules too. Rules protect them and give them parameters to experiment with their freedom in the safety of their parents' love and concern. ADD children also need a solid regular routine. They thrive on structure and the predictable.

Rules for our children should be easy to understand and logical. They should not be arbitrary and open to different interpretations. Well thought out rules provide safety for children and remove us from constantly nagging. For instance, if you have a house rule that states if anyone does not do a chore the consequence is added chores, then you should have chores ready to be assigned. You should have a ready list of monthly, quarterly or yearly household tasks. You do not have to nag and cajole your daughter to take out the garbage; simply point out to her the next morning that she must choose a chore from the chore jar.

Rules should be very simple and not open to vague interpretation. They work best if expressed positively and if they give a child a positive action they can concentrate on achieving. For instance, instead of saying, "no running in Dad's workshop," the rule is best expressed by saying, "we walk carefully and slowly in Dad's workshop." This keeps the desired behavior before the child. Consequences should also be clear and there should be room for redemption. For instance, a child should not be banned from Dad's workshop all day simply because he was running. He might have to leave for a short while then return after he has calmed down. Household rules are needed for ADD children because they need parameters. Rules help them to feel safe and secure.

Rules should reflect how you want the physical and spiritual environment to be in your home. ADD children need to know social as well as environmental rules. For instance, in our home respecting that each family member was made in the image of God means we do not call one another names. It also means we respect the place we call home and keep it orderly. The rules reflect the peaceful atmosphere I want in our home as well as the environment I want my children to grow up in. In some homes, the dwelling is immaculate but the atmosphere is harsh and judgmental. You can actually feel it when you walk in and that sour spiritual atmosphere takes away from any beauty that might be in the physical environment.

Make simple rules that represent character traits you want to see developed in your family. Kindness might be a rule. It is very easy to say we are a kind family so we are kind to one another and to our possessions so we do not jump up and down on the sofa or beat the table with our light saber. House rules that encourage organization and teamwork are a necessity in every family. Complying to rules is important for our children as they need to develop good habits. Habits are behaviors that last a lifetime because habits are behaviors we do instinctively. Good habits guarantee our good behavior and therefore success.

Good habits can only be formed through repetition or routine. Routines, like rules, provide emotional and physical security for your child. A routine is just a schedule. The schedule should not be rigid. Routines can be done very easily by just asking yourself what you generally do (or want to do) daily. Post the routine. Use clip art or magazine pictures and your children will get an additional visual reminder. A copy of the daily schedule can be placed in your child's room and the kitchen. Eventually reliance on the posted list will diminish as the child forms good habits based on repetition.

Parents should ideally have a morning, afternoon (after school) and evening/bedtime routine. You may also have checklists, or routines for going to a place of worship, the store or the babysitter. The routines help to direct your child in the rules. By having the rules and routines written out, you can ensure that everyone is aware of the next item on the day's agenda. This gives your child the opportunity to prepare proactively for each day. Posted rules are reminders for our children.

Rules are not just to gain a child's obedience and to make parenting easy; an effective rule serves the child long term. For instance, you do not let your child have dessert before dinner, not just to conform him to a social norm, but to help him develop healthy eating habits that you hope will last a lifetime. Your child needs reinforcement and affirmation for adhering to the rules. Generally, we only notice when our children break the rules but we must reward our child for rule compliance.

Rewards go a long way for reinforcing a desired behavior. You might reward your child for cleaning her bedroom. Some parents may not agree with rewarding a child for household tasks. However, I generally point out to parents that good habits have to be reinforced and a short-term reward for a continued clean room can help establish habitual room cleaning. Once this habit is firmly established the child can be slowly weaned off the reward and you can direct your attention to other habits you would like to see become more automatic to them.

You can also reward the child with a family game night, or points from chores can accumulate such that the family can go on a vacation when a certain number have been earned. Chore charts that promise a specific reward or privilege at the week's completion work best with most children. Promising your child a surprise for the completion of a chore can backfire if your child does not consider the award worthy of the chore completed. Some parents tie a child's allowance to the completion of chores. Others give family privileges like pizza night if all chores are done in excellence. A task must not be done shabbily or haphazardly to receive a reward. We want our children to understand and value hard work. This is often a daily lesson we must teach them.

Daily rules and routines are a safe place of predictability for children. It secures them emotionally. Your daily schedule should be clear and predictable yet flexible. You need not schedule every activity to the microsecond, yet at the same time if you are too vague your child will be unsettled by the lack of structure. All children find security in structure but children with ADD find it quite unnerving to be in an environment that is ever changing without rhyme or reason.

Rules also help siblings to understand inherently that you want to be fair with everyone and are not just compensating for an ADD sibling. Sometimes in our zeal to manage the behavior of our ADD child our other children get lost in the shuffle. Clear rules and routines help all our children to know we genuinely care about them. Rules are our expectations of our children and studies show clearly that our children will live up to our expectations. Our children need to know that they will be given guidance and respect with rules. Our children need help and depend on us to give them rules that will guide them into good habits and organized behavior.

Rules are best enforced if they occur within a routine. A routine is not negotiable with ADD children. Even the most disorganized parent has a routine or structure. That parent may not like his routine but there are certain predictable tasks he does every day nonetheless. Sometimes many of us are just so overwhelmed with dealing with our children's day-to-day challenges that we have developed more of a sur-vival mentality. We say to ourselves, "If I can just get through today I'll be happy." The problem with this kind of thinking is that we barely keep our heads above the proverbial crisis wave and lose the joy of parenting in the process when con-stantly dealing with our children's emotional, behavioral and academic struggles.

A good routine works for everyone involved including you! If I were to take you through a full-time management exercise, I would have you write your goals and break them down into smaller steps such that you have the ability to work on them daily. Generally, our daily schedules should be governed by our personal and professional goals or else we get stifled into crisis mode. In a crisis mode we expel effort spinning our wheels or putting out one fire then another be-cause we are only dealing in the here and now. It is essential for us to see beyond today and into tomorrow.

Most books and time management programs advise us parents to start early in the morning and to plan our day forward. This is not a good option if you have a child with ADD, impulse and focus issues because the truth is we can-not think clearly until they are in bed and out of commission for the night. It is generally at this time that you can relax and plan. Thus I suggest you work backwards to create a realistic schedule. What time would you like your child to go to bed? Choose a time that is realistic, keeping in mind that if your child is on medication she may be challenged in her appetite and as a result dinner may be a bit more prolonged than you might want it to be. Rather than get angry with this fact, just add time to your scheduled dinner hour. Of course, this does not preclude discussing dosage alternatives with your child's doctors. I am merely pointing out that you might want to be more realistic in your schedule when as-signing time periods.

Broadly schedule your day. Provide your child some free time. I know for some of you this seems strange. After all, doesn't your child need structure? Yes, he does, but structure does not preclude enjoyable activities for your child. In fact, planning regular intervals of enjoyable activities will motivate your child to attend to unpleasant tasks. An important element of time management, which cannot be ignored, is preparation time. Preparation time must be scheduled in many activities because our children need time to transition into new activities.

Preparation is key when making a schedule, thus creating a routine for your child. Bedtime is also a process. Many parent/child bedtime issues have more to do with poor planning and preparation than anything else. Bedtime is more than just brushing teeth and grabbing a cuddly teddy bear. It is a key transitional time for your child.

Transitions are particularly challenging for children with attention and focus issues. It is unsettling and therefore this needs to be a particularly predictable and pleasant time. Plan some quiet activity like listening to calming music or a story on CD or cassette, if you are too tired to read to your child. Choose books with calming themes. Jim Weiss, a master and award-winning storyteller, has written some great children's classics and bedtime stories that even middle schoolers (ages 10–14) will enjoy (visit http://greathall.com for an exhaustive list of his audiobooks). His stories are dramatic enough to hold children's attention and are unabridged. They are also a good resource to help with your child's reading. Our family enjoys his material immensely. His captivating voice also holds children's attention and yet in his bedtime stories the tone is appropriate such that children are not riled up when they should be relaxing. Listening to a story is an enjoyable activity and helps children transition more easily. You can also play calming classical music. There is a whole list of suggested useful resources at the end of this book.

Routine and rules are a major component of organizing your ADD child. Fun and individuality must be balanced with rules. The rules and routine also must not be complicated. They must be simple. In the next chapter, we will discuss simplicity.

FURTHER TIPS

- Use a sticker chart as an incentive to get your child to pick up his toys or do his chores. A full sticker chart may be redeemed for a family treat like an extra hour of television or games. Print out reward certificates from your computer or purchase them in a teacher or office supply store and once a month give out rewards for household chores well done. Make a chore chart and post smiley faces near a child's completed tasks.

- Make cut outs of stars and give them out to children when they help you with various household chores. Children may also trade stars with their siblings in return for help with chores. Stars can be redeemed for family prizes like an afternoon with Mom or Dad.

- Assign points to the household tasks in your home. Require each child to do chores worth an agreed number of points. Draw chores out of a container for tasks that have pre-assigned points. Family members can all perform their chosen chores.

- Post calendars in kids' rooms, especially small children who do not have a concept of time. They can cross off the days until a special event occurs. You can also have them make the calendars themselves, once a month. Older children might enjoy getting character or hobby related calendars.

4 Keep It Simple and Specific

The fourth step in the F.I.R.S.T. method is to keep organizing simple and specific for our children. We parents often get sidetracked in our efforts to help our children. At times we overcomplicate very simple things. ADD children also need simple instructions that are specific and direct. It is essential we give children short easy directions/instructions no matter what the task.

Use broad and basic terms that can be applied to different situations. For instance, when my children were small we used to say "put it in its home", meaning put a misplaced item back where it belongs. "Put it in its home" is a term you can use to remind your child to hang up her coat or to put her toys away or even to remind her to put completed homework in her homework folder. Put it in its home is an easy concept for children to understand in a wide variety of contexts and settings. This is especially helpful for ADD children who often have difficulty transferring skills to different environments. This term can also be used for the child to remind himself to put his school papers back where they belong.

Our language needs to be very basic and brief when giving our children directions. Sometimes we speak so much that our children just tune us out. Our vocabulary should be simple and specific. Children younger than eight are highly distractible and will often forget what you tell them to do if a significant time lapse occurs. For instance, if you send your son outside to get the newspaper but the child is distracted by your neighbor's friendly golden retriever and he goes over to pet the dog, he will easily forget the newspaper.

Keep it simple. Use one sentence, for instance say, "Go and get the newspaper." Ask the child to repeat back to you what he is going to do. A dynamic occurs in the brain when the child says, "I am going to get the newspaper." He is less likely to be distracted when he articulates what he is going to do. You might also provide him with a clue to remember what he was sent to do. For instance, you might give your child a peg to remember to give to you when he returns with the newspaper. You can make a memory stick out of an old toy or wooden spoon. It can be used to remind your child to get the newspaper for you. The memory stick can be returned to you when the child gives you the newspaper. The memory stick keeps you from using many words and helps your child to remember what you asked him to do.

Sometimes we may perceive an act as disobedience when our children just did not remember what was said to them. Always speak in simple declarative sentences or what I call "one-step directives" with a verb that's something easy for them to do. You want to say, "Pick up the paper off the floor." You don't want to give your child a long lecture about why the floor has to be sanitary and the benefits of a well-ordered home. Your child will tune out your paper diatribe.

Most children can only perform one verbal instruction, or step directives in a simple three step ordered sequence with context for the child. The instructions are easier to follow if they are simple and make sense to the child. Some children can handle two- to three-word directives as long as it is still given in a three step sequential manner. For instance, if you're telling your child to get ready for bed then the tasks you tell him to do should revolve around the bedtime ritual.

It would not be a good time to discuss a scouting trip two weeks away when you have given the child three bedtime-related tasks to do. The bedtime routine will help your child remember bedtime tasks.

On a very simplistic level, every task we give our children must make sense to them. They must derive some understanding or appreciation for what we are asking them to do or else the task seems abstract to the child. Every task should be relevant to the child. A two year old likes dressing himself and doing things for himself; therefore he will enjoy hanging up his own coat because he wants to be independent. The chore is relevant to him. It serves him in some way. Requiring a child to place school notes in a folder is important to the child only if the child understands the urgency of returning notes and the consequences of notes that are not returned.

Simplicity is synonymous with ease for a child. Make it easy for your child to comply with your requests. Place hooks at your child's eye level, so she can easily and effortlessly hang up her jackets. Get simple bedding for your child's room so she can make the bed without your assistance. Put the vacuum cleaner in an easily accessible place so that when cereal spills it is easy to locate. Keep your chore charts large and uncluttered so children can easily read them. Your family calendar should be posted in a place your child is likely to see/read it. We merely need to ask ourselves if we have made complying with our requests simple and easy for our children.

Label everything to keep life simple for your child. Put your child's name on his books and papers. I found that when children are given pencils with their names on them they kept up with them better than just the standard pencils. Labeling or identifying a child's possessions is very easy to do. My kids used to argue over whose sweat socks were whose until I wrote their initials on the bottom of their socks with indelible ink. I also did this on my kids' swimsuits, ballet outfits and coats. You can catch indelible laundry markers on sale during back-to-school sales but they are also widely available at most chain discount stores. Labeling takes the mystery out of wondering whose sock is in the middle of the living room floor. It also relieves a child's stress of bringing home the wrong belongings from school.

Simplicity seems so basic to adults that we sometimes fail to realize the abstract terms we use with our children. "Clean your room" is abstract for children. Clean is a vague term that means different things to different people. Define clean for your child. Be very specific what you define as clean. If possible make a written and pictorial list for your child. One mom I know actually cleaned up her children's rooms and took pictures with her digital camera. She then enlarged them and gave them to her children so they both were working from the same definition of clean. Her children knew specifically what was required of them. This made cleaning their rooms simple.

Besides a simple list or graphic representation, ADD children need time in between tasks so that they do not get overwhelmed. For instance, when guiding your child to clean her room, survey the items that need to be organized in the room. Typically, children have toys, books, paper and clothes in their rooms that need to be organized. You might instruct a child to go and pick up all the clothes in her room and either hang them up, or place them in the hamper. After the child has picked up all the clothing, move on to the next item. The more specific we are with our children the more cooperation we will get from them. A "clean your room" list should only have a few items on it. For young children the list should include no more than five or six items. If necessary, help little ones clean their room so you can train them at the same time to do the difficult specifics of the task.

Specifics are essential to children because they are often paralyzed when we are too vague. A child has to know exactly what is expected of him or he will become discouraged and stop trying to be successful. Do not overcomplicate anything. When making checklists and family rules keep them simple and brief. Sometimes we ask our children to do things that are just too difficult for them. For instance, we insist they hang up their coats but they cannot easily reach the hooks. Part of making it easy for children is just to make it easy to perform the task. If you want them to put away their sports equipment then have a place for them to put it when they come in hot and sweaty after a game. Hooks work great because they can hold jackets, backpacks and caps. Make the hooks child eye level; then the child can place almost anything on them. Do you have an inbox for notes when your child comes home from school or soccer practice?

Children also need to be able to see visually what must be done; therefore, it is imperative that chore charts are at their eye level, not yours. They should also be visually appealing for children, but do not clutter the charts making them too cutesy. Your child can only focus in on a few words at a time. You can create chore charts on the computer or purchase them. (See the list of chores on pp.115–118.) The important thing is that you post your child's daily chores list so that it is always before him. I have also found that many ADD children need the added memory jog of a pictorial representation of any task they had to do. For instance, if they are to take out the garbage a picture of a trash can (either sketched or cut out from a magazine) would be appropriate. Since we remember in pictures, it is easier for them to associate the task with the time if a visual representation of the task is located near the assigned task on the chore chart. In addition, all family chores should have a scheduled time for action and completion. Chore time should be posted in your child's planner.

Besides chore charts, our family and many clients have found checklists are indispensable. Checklists are basically routines that are written down. In our family, we have morning checklists that include teeth brushing, face washing, etc., and other vital hygiene activities. Older children or tweens are embarrassed about you making inquiries about their deodorant usage or whether or not they brushed their teeth, etc., so it is helpful just to be able to ask, "Have you done the Morning checklist?" One family I know has an exit checklist because they found someone was always forgetting something until they posted an exit checklist by the door.

Checklists are merely sequential reminders. Parents have told me that they utilize morning checklists to help with the morning chaos. Our family has a nighttime checklist to ensure everyone goes to bed without delay and at the same time prepares for the next day. Checklists should be posted but they do not have to be placed on the wall—even though at one time our morning and nightly checklist were posted in the kids' bathroom because they really needed to see it daily—they can be placed in a family book or laminated and kept in a drawer until needed. I found that as my children got older they did not want their visiting friends and extended family to know about their routines.

Laminated checklists with pictorial cues or symbols are especially effective for young children and ADD youngsters because holding the checklist in their hands provides the added benefit of tactile sensory input. Checklists also give children security and structure, which they instinctually crave. If a child is to use laminated checklists, you will have to work with the child to return the checklists to their designated place or home.

Children need to develop good habits and this can only happen as a result of forming good habits. Good habits can only be formed through repetition. Checklists work best to create routines and repetition. This also cements a child to the structure. Checklists can be written out, pictures may be used with small children, or both words and visual cues may be used to reinforce the checklists. I still give out checklists to the teens with whom I work. Contracts are "formal signed agreements between you and your child." Contracts can be made on what constitutes a clean room, completed home-work, etc.

ADD children think better in environments that are not overtly stimulating such as bright and bold colors, yet at the same time a boring white wall does not engage them either. Keeping your home decorated simply and giving specific and distinct purposes to each room will help your child to concentrate. Keeping your home and your communication with your child simple and specific will engender the most cooperation from your child. Utilizing fun with firmness while addressing a child's individuality and interests, along with a strong set of rules relating to a regular routine, all rests on us being specific and keeping it simple with our children.

FURTHER TIPS

- Use a flow chart like a drawn racetrack so your child can visually mark his progress in a task. I once used a racetrack with young children to show them they were progressing toward their goals. They advanced the car for each step they made toward their reading goals.

- Place hobby or interest-related calendars in your tween's room. They will use anything they can personally relate to.

- Encourage your child to make a to-do list for a special project. Ask him to estimate the time it will take to complete each task. You can do this by simply taking a big sheet of paper and writing down the top three things you have to do to accomplish the project. Use index cards to record each step so that your child can focus on one task at a time.

- Use the wall space to store items in your child's room to organize their toys and clothing. Shelves and poster board can be mounted on the walls.

- Many kids like to throw their things. Hang a basketball hoop over their hamper or over a laundry basket to collect worn clothing. There are ready-made hanging hampers that work the same way.

5 Address Time and Transitions

Managing time is an imperative skill for children. ADD children are no exception; in fact they need to regulate their time more stringently because they have to watch for transitions in their time. Transitions are troublesome for ADD children who thrive on predictability and routine because they require them to do a mind shift. Shifting quickly from one activity to the other is not easy for ADD children; therefore these times need to be planned for in advance.

Children with impulse issues are prone to "act out" during transitional times. It is essential when scheduling your day to note whenever there is a change from one activity to the other, then to be certain you provide space for your child to make the mental and emotional shift before he physically has to move from one activity to the other. Simply give the child a warning such as "in five minutes we will be having dinner." Your child will probably need more than one reminder. The reminders can also be a learned response. For instance, you could put on music when it is dinnertime and when your child hears the music he can prepare to shift from playing to preparing for dinner. The music becomes his transitional cue.

Transitional cues have many advantages. Your child cannot argue or tantrum with a musical cue. She is obliged simply to come to the table. Another excellent transitional technique is to use movement. Stretch or dance (if your child is young and doesn't think it is too silly) to the next room where you want the child to go. You might combine music with movement and put on a clean-up song when it is time for him to put away his game to move to the next activity. Older children will generally prefer to stretch or do light exercises.

Transitional objects also can be used. I have used transitional objects successfully with students. It also works well with young children. You can designate a teddy bear (or other inanimate object) Mister Time to Make a Change Bear. You can hand your child the bear when she has to change activities. You might also want to tell your child to teach the bear to stop, think and then proceed to the next activity. You can use a ruler or compass or any other appropriate item with older children. This will reinforce when you want the child to stop, think and then proceed to the next activity. Teaching the bear will reinforce how to make transitions and older children would appreciate the tangible reminder of a compass.

It may seem silly to use a stuffed animal or a compass but learning to transition is a major skill and achievement for ADD children. Transitional time issues often plague people with ADD into adulthood and the sooner they learn to compensate for their weakness the better off they will be. All of us have weaknesses and we become stronger and more accomplished as we each learn to compensate for those weaknesses. It is imperative that you identify times of transition in your schedule so you can help your child engage in planning for those times.

It seems like a great deal of work to deal with such moments in the short term but if transition times are not planned, it can ruin much of your long-term planning because it requires you to deal needlessly with tantrums and emotional upsets. One intense emotional upset can throw the whole family off kilter. Transitional times are no small issue for ADD children. Carefully examine your family and child's schedule and plan for transitional times.

ADD children need to manage their long-term goals. Sometimes parents and children get so involved in the day-to-day they forget to help their children make long-term plans. Time cannot be managed adequately until you and your child make some goals because time management is just managing the events of our lives. Goals keep all of us future oriented and out of the muck and mire of everyday living. Successful people are goal oriented. Studies show that those who make goals and work toward them are happier and more well adjusted than the average population.

Teach your child early the importance of goals and how to pursue goals. Explain to your child a goal is a wish that they want to see come true. Goals should be specific, measurable, attainable, realistic and have a designated time for accomplishment. The book *A Kid's Guide to Organizing* by Jarret, Janae and Jolene Carter has a complete goal process you can go through with your children. It is specifically written to children and will direct you in the process. Once you have gone through the goal process with your child, write the goals on 5x8 index cards and put pictures on them. If your child is young, have him draw a picture on the back of the card about how he will feel once the goal is accomplished. This makes the goal real to your child and motivates him to achieve. You may also ask the child to close his eyes and actually see himself achieving the goal.

The goal will be a motivator for your child. Break the goals down into manageable chunks that translate into daily tasks. Turn these daily tasks into a realistic schedule. Write a schedule for your child with a bedtime and a rising time. Help your child set a bedtime routine for herself that will help her achieve her goals. Encourage her to get her clothes out the night before school and to pack her backpack. Provide her with a checklist she can follow every night. Compose the checklist on construction paper or brightly colored

8½ x 11 paper and remember to include visual reminders (use clip art, line drawings or magazine pictures) on the checklist. Laminate the checklist. This gives it a sense of permanency and reality for the child. Put the goals on the back of the laminated checklist paper so your child sees how her goals relate to her daily schedule.

Your child should be encouraged to make school goals. This has a twofold effect. It will make school more interesting and the ADD child will be able to concentrate if he has a goal and it is a realistic goal the child can honestly achieve. School goals will be accomplished as the child develops good study habits. Designate a quiet, well-lit area in your home for studying. Get your child a "do not disturb" sign for her bedroom door when she is studying. If your home is noisy, take your child to the library. It is important the child sees how seriously you regard her education. Encourage your child to sit upright at a table or desk as opposed to slouching in a comfy chair or lying across the bed.

Goals will help your child take responsibility. As much as possible allow your child to take responsibility for his time as well. Get your child an alarm clock. You can get a variety of children's alarm clocks to reflect their personality. Set a wake-up time for your child. You may have to help little ones with the concept of getting up and responding to an alarm clock. After your child gets up have him follow a simple morning checklist. Place the alarm clock for older children away from their bed so that they have to get up and turn off the alarm. This will prevent them from hitting the snooze function on the alarm clock. There are also a myriad of alarm clocks with extra loud alarms and moving and flying alarm clocks as well. (See the list of useful resources.)

When planning with your child, schedule extra time for homework. ADD children need to take breaks during long concentrated periods such as homework. Give your child a break by having her stretch, play a musical instrument or stroke the family pet for about five minutes to break up the monotony of homework. Set a homework routine for your child. At the beginning of the school year, get rid of any old papers so your child has a fresh start. Get separate colored folders for your child. Designate folders for school notes, homework and graded papers. Middle-school students (ages 10–14) will need files for each subject. By having these files at home your child will easily be able to file the random papers in his backpack immediately when he gets home. Encourage young children to bring all their papers home so you can file them. Toss old papers for your child but hold onto old tests to review and for cumulative exams. Weekly, go through your child's bag/home desk and toss outdated notes, and old assignments.

Managing time necessitates your child having a planner. A planner helps your child master her time. Most schools give out planners but few teachers really take the time to ensure ADD students know how to use them. The ones that have pocket folders, dividers and planning calendars are ideal. (See the suggested useful resources list at the back of the book.) Some traditional school planners are just too busy for ADD students. The boxes are too small to write in and the planners do not delineate time periods enough for ADD students.

Typically, ADD students need large boxes and lots of white space without distracting photos or pictures. The planner does not have to be plain but decorations are a distraction. I recommend teacher plan books or specialty planners. Emphasize the importance of using a planner with your child. Your children should use one calendar for school, extracurricular and home activities. When more than one calendar is used, the risk of scheduling conflicts, missed appointments and over-scheduling occurs. You might want to consider color-coding similar activities on your child's calendar. Your child may use highlighters or colored pencils to indicate school, home and recreational activities. ADD children in particular need to realize that school affects every area of their lives.

The planner should be wide ruled for young children with a month at a glance and the ability to see assignments on a weekly basis and not just on a daily basis. ADD children need lots of space to write assignments. The difficulties with handwriting also dictate that the planner has lots of space for children to write assignments. When children only document things on a daily basis, they fail to develop big-picture thinking. It is essential that in addition to the planners being easy to use you check them daily until recording in the planner becomes routine or habit for children. Keep reviewing your child's planner with them until it becomes a habit.

Key exams and projects should be indicated in the planner. Encourage your child to make a study plan for an exam as soon as the exam is announced. Study time should be a regular part of your child's schedule, separate and distinct from homework time. Good students know study time must be a regular part of their schedule. Show your children how to break up major school projects into smaller more manageable parts. For instance, if they have to read two chapters they can easily read portions of those chapters over a week. They can also take notes on the chapters. Reward your children for managing their time well.

Finally, since time and organizational issues will persist with ADD children, I recommend every family have a time management and organizing center. The center should be stocked with planner pages and time management tools. This will be discussed further in the next chapter. Suffice to say, you must model good time management skills for your child. Post a family calendar in a prominent place in your home. Refer often to your schedule and regularly practice good time management skills. Your child will want to use a planner if he sees you using a planner. Fun, individuality, rules, simplicity and time all mesh together to help us organize our children. In the next section we will look at how this is implemented in school.

FURTHER TIPS

- Create a time management/study learning center in your home. Post classes, calendar, tests, trips, birthdays and special lessons. Post dates to refresh class supplies (such as pencils, pens, crayons, etc.) on the family calendar and in your child's planner/organizer/calendar in the time management center.

- Every child needs a planner. Consider getting an electronic one if necessary but remember you will need to train your child in its use and provide follow-up and feedback until using it becomes habit.

- Purchase or create a family calendar that is posted so that your child sees that managing your time is important to all and that no one person in the family is more important than another.

- Make an ideal schedule for your family—that is what each person in the family would like the schedule to be, despite how often we fall short of our best intentions. This can be a sobering realization for both parents and children.

6 Plan for School Success

Once you have implemented most of the F.I.R.S.T. organizing tools and generally your child is acclimated to routines and habitually using her planner you can move on to her organizational skills at school. Disorganized kids can usually compensate somewhat during the elementary years (ages 5–10) when parents and teachers primarily put organizing structures in place. By middle school (ages 10–14), students are expected to have their own organizing game plan in place. Some children do but most are simply hoisted into new classes and such broad responsibilities that they simply never catch up with those expectations. This is why it's of primary importance that children, particularly ADD students, be instructed in organizational skills as early as possible and not merely told what to do. An explanation as to why they are doing it should be provided.

You can begin the process at home almost immediately by having a homework routine. Your child should have a well-lit area in which to study. Depending on your child's personality, he may want to work at his own desk, or some very social children prefer the kitchen table. It is important that children have good posture while doing homework or handwriting will be sloppy. This is especially important for school-aged children. It also helps to allow your child to squeeze a stress ball or other malleable object to relieve her stress and to help her sit and focus during homework time. ADD children should also be placed in an area where they are not easily distracted. For instance, next to a window, a high traffic area, or one with lots of background noise would not be a good choice.

Some parents have even placed children in homemade cubicles to reduce distractions. While theoretically this is a good idea, it can also be restricting to children to only have a cut-out box to look at all the time. This should only be used in extreme cases. If you attach Velcro to the cubicle, you may also post your child's vocabulary words or number facts or interesting yet relaxing pictures such as a babbling brook. If you do opt to use a cubicle make sure that you give your child breaks in between subjects or segments of work so she can walk around, pet the dog, play an instrument, etc. Fifteen minutes, at the most 20 minutes, is tops when it comes to sitting down and focusing on any task. Another trick many of my ADD parents have used is to have their children sniff a little lemon juice or peppermint; the scent seems to help children focus.

A well-lit comfortable desk coupled with a homework routine will ensure homework does not take all night. I usually suggest to families that they establish a specified homework time and adhere to it daily. Generally, if your child knows homework time is daily from 3 pm to 5 pm he will get in the habit of doing his homework the same time every day, thus you should encounter less resistance. In addition, on days when he has no instructor-assigned schoolwork, he can use that time to study. You may need to clean or encourage your child to keep a clean desk. A bulletin board also will allow your child to see items he may be prone to forget.

It helps if the whole family is doing some kind of studying, reading or meditative work at the agreed-upon study or quiet time. Your child's desk should be free of extraneous papers. You can put a small file on the desk to place papers in instead of his backpack. All your child's needed supplies, including pens, pencils, compass, rulers, calculator, etc., should be filed neatly on his desk. If your child does not have a desk then you should have these items in a homework box. You may also provide coloring books and small manipulative toys for younger siblings who are not doing homework or who complete assignments quickly. This keeps everyone doing quiet work at the same time even if a sibling has no homework.

I also recommend that parents get the enrichment books that cover subjects in grades K–8 (ages 5–14) to review subject areas on days when a brother or sister needs quiet. Also, encourage your child to take a brief break from homework and eat healthy snacks like peanuts, peaches, etc., which are known to be food for the brain. The US Department of Agriculture (USDA) has found that foods like these feed our brains (see www.ars.usda.gov/is/ar/archive/aug07/aging0807.htm).

Many parents wonder how much help they should give their children. We parents are coaches. Besides telling them to tackle the hardest subject first and some brief guidance to be certain they have everything they need, we should not intervene unless they specifically ask for help. Even that request should be met with a pep talk and a pat on the back after minimal assistance is given. If your child truly does not understand an assignment, the teacher needs to know or perhaps the child needs a tutor. Also, at times we think our children don't understand the homework when in fact they just don't understand the instructions. Read the instructions with your child before she starts her homework. Tell her to picture, to get an image in her head, of what the directions are asking her to do. For instance, if the child is to circle all the rhyming words have the child picture a circle and even draw a circle in the air before settling down to tackle the homework.

Homework should also be balanced with physical activity. Take your child to the park, play ball or go to the movies, once the homework is completed. She will appreciate the reward, and understand that hard work pays off. In addition, be certain your child is stretching or doing some sort of physical activity between subjects. Your son may spend 15 minutes doing math homework; then ask him to do something physical. I like to couple it with household chores so occasionally when working with parents I suggest the child gallop up to his bedroom and pick up as many toys as he can off the floor in ten minutes. A timer would be necessary. After ten minutes, he could do a brief breathing or relaxation exercise, then move on to the next assignment.

Some teens will insist they can do their homework while lounging on the floor or their bed. This is not a good idea because posture and body position are important when concentrating. They will actually finish their homework faster and will naturally be more alert when sitting up in an attentive posture. They will disagree but if you challenge them to try it your way for a week they might be convinced. Couple your way with some other ideas including light baroque music played while they study. Baroque music, in particular the artists Bach, Handel, Vivaldi and Corelli, appears to help students concentrate because it pulses between 50 and 80 beats per minute and this pattern seems to stabilize our mental, physical and emotional processes. Try borrowing some pieces from your local library before you invest in a particular artist. Some classroom teachers regularly use concentration music to help students to calm down and focus.

Managing papers can be hard. It is best to use three-ring binders, not individual spiral notebooks. Your child might be resistant to this at first but if you allow him to design the front of his binders he might be more willing. Color-code your child's notebooks with his folders. The folders should be three-hole-punched then placed inside the binders. High-school students (ages 14–18) should have different color one-inch binders for each class. These binders can be subdivided into class notes, homework, graded work or exams and reference notes (e.g. formulas you have memorized for math or foreign language). Your middle-schooler (ages 10–14) should carry a portable three-hole punch in her backpack and/or locker so she can immediately hole-punch paper when given to her and place it in the correct folder. They are readily available and lightweight because so many students carry them.

Remember to connect home and school: a corresponding file retrieval system should be set up at home where the papers can be placed after each quarter or marking period. Some students prefer to use spiral notebooks. If your child is resistant to using a binder then he can just record class notes in three-hole color-coordinated notebooks then place them in his subdivided binders. Young children can have separate sections within their notebooks, with their folders likewise color coordinated with three ring holes punched. Rather than getting regular dividers, get dividers that double as folders as well. You will need to check your child's notebook weekly to ensure the papers are promptly filed at home. Of course, when the school year is over all those files can be tossed unless your child is moving to another school or you need to document a year's progress.

Another key to management is to be certain your child can do things quickly. To ensure papers are not just tossed haphazardly in their school bag place a three-hole-punched pencil case fixed neatly in the front of their binder. This should contain pens, pencils and a portable three-hole puncher to secure assignments immediately. You can give him a regular 5x7 pencil case to remain in his desk or school locker. You can also purchase locker shelves, drawers and other accessories so that your child's locker does not become a black hole. Also, if your child tends to forget to bring home the necessary textbooks try color coding the books. Cover them with different color covers, then make strips of paper or laminate colored cards to correspond to those books. When your child is assigned a lesson in a particular class she simply has to move the card to the front of her notebook/binder and perhaps place it in a clear hole-punched pencil case. At the end of the day before leaving school, she can look at the cards and pack the textbooks needed instead of trying to remember each book.

It is imperative that your child makes the connection between studying at home and success in school. Successful students realize their lives are lived holistically. On the first day of school, photocopy your child's class syllabus and class schedule. Keep a copy at home; affix one inside your child's backpack and the other in his locker. This is critical for ADD students. Also, put study planning sheets in your child's planner. (See the form templates at the back of the book.) I also recommend a time management center be established at home to include time management sheets, goal planning and study or project planning. I generally recommend the clear plastic six drawer units that are sold in popular discount stores. If you choose to get a storage dresser without transparent drawers you should label the drawers so the child knows what is in each one without opening it. They are usually on sale around back-to-school time and in January when people are making New Year's resolutions to get more organized.

It is a good idea to follow up most school assignments with some sort of multi-sensory exercise. When your child has spelling words you can have her write them out in the air with you before she sits down to do a worksheet. Movement really does help the brain to engage and it is a good idea to couple movement with schoolwork. You can have your child bounce a ball reciting his addition number facts before doing his math homework. Movement can also be followed by relaxation exercises. You can have your child breathe deeply from the diaphragm, not the lungs like most of us do. To ensure he is doing it correctly, have him place his hand on his belly button: when he breathes in his stomach should contract and when he breathes out it should spread. He can do this five times, and follow this with a positive affirmation such as "Homework is easy for me. I finish it quickly, accurately and completely." Then your child is ready both mentally and physically to concentrate on homework.

Scholastics is just one area in which our children have to apply their organizational skills. In the next chapter we will specifically look at your child's environment because an uncluttered environment is necessary for uncluttered thoughts.

FURTHER TIPS

- Set up a filing cabinet for older children. File information by class, keeping a section for tests or notes that may be used later in cumulative finals.

- Write a note to your child's teacher suggesting scheduling a weekly clean-your-desk time for the whole class. Offer to provide rewards for the classmates who comply.

- Post educational or family goals in special journals. Refer to them monthly or quarterly. This motivates students to achieve goals and provides accountability because the whole family knows about the goal. Encourage your child to do this with his friends as well.

- Get your school-age child an organizer/planner and show her how to use it. Make certain it is wide ruled for young children with a month at a glance and the ability to view their assignments on a weekly basis and not just on a daily basis. When children only document things on a daily basis, they fail to develop big-picture thinking. They will also need you to review it with them until it becomes a habit.

7 Your Child's Bedroom

AN UNCLUTTERED ENVIRONMENT— TACKLING YOUR CHILD'S BEDROOM

One of the major areas in which your child needs order is his immediate environment. A child's bedroom can be a major battleground because it is the place the child wants to accentuate his personality yet the parent wants to see order. Remember, children are naturally evolving into their own persons and separating themselves from us so it should come as no surprise that a child's bedroom can become a major issue. Let's look at it from your youngster's perspective. Her room reflects her personality and individuality. It is the one place in her small world where she can be herself. So while you see the mess, she sees her home. This is not to suggest that children do not enjoy order, because they do, but they do not necessarily enjoy order that is imposed on them in a way that does not respect them as individuals.

With the understanding that we must respect our children's space, let's take a fresh look at their rooms. Also inherent in this discussion would be the question of what constitutes clean as defined by a parent. You may need to sit down with your child to determine an agreed definition of clean that both of you can live with. As trite as that sounds that may be what is causing most of the disorder in your child's room. My teen son had me sign an agreement regarding what I precisely want when I ask him to clean his room. This was very helpful because I realized some of the perceived messes in his room were part of his personality and I had to respect that. For instance, if your child enjoys putting together jigsaw puzzles over a few weeks and the only space available is the floor but you want the floor to be clean you are going to have conflict. Reduce conflict by talking about why messes may occur. Do not just accuse your child of being lazy, indifferent or just uncaring.

Do not assume the worst about your child. Young children may simply be too overwhelmed with their possessions to keep their bedrooms tidy. They need help, but as we have discussed, since a child is always developmentally moving toward autonomy she will probably not ask for assistance. Offer to lend a helping hand. Do not take over the process but serve as a coach. Encourage your child to purge their bedroom of clutter. This is the first step to maintaining a clean environment. Getting a child to release clutter is going to be very difficult.

ADD children tend to be hoarders. They have difficulty separating who they are from what they have—their possessions. In fact, some children find it exceptionally hard to share in part because they have a need to feel unique. It is just an innate part of childhood that our children collect everything from plastic yogurt spoons to worn pointless pencils. By the time your child is a tween (ages 9–12) they are collecting CDs, magazines, crafts, comics, computer games, books, etc. These items hold memories for them and are part of them establishing themselves as individuals with interests separate and distinct from us. Be careful not to refer to these prized collections as junk or useless.

We cannot just go in our child's room and make it like we want it to be; it should be a reflection of who the child is, therefore it must be functional for your child. This is why it is vitally important to sit down with your child and compromise on what is acceptable. The room ultimately has to be a place you both can live with but your child really has to be able to feel at home in his own room. It must reflect him. I can hear you already: but what if your child's room is a complete disaster? Then you do have to intervene, ever so lovingly and with the utmost respect for your child.

The first thing you will do after speaking with your child is to arrange a time when you can both tackle the task together. Go in the room armed with three large garbage bags labeled Put Away, Give Away and Throw Away. Pretend you are the hands of a clock and rotate around the room clockwise picking up every item. Ask your child which bag the item should be placed in. Prod your child along as she may not be comfortable throwing anything away at first. If children share a room, delve into this task with both of them. You might also want to get boxes instead of bags for young children. I use file boxes for young children because they can easily see what is going in each box and it shows you are honoring their decisions because the child can look in a box and easily retrieve an item if he changes his mind. A child should have the right to reverse a decision, and an open box the child can easily see into as opposed to a closed trash bag sometimes makes all the difference to the child. It shows you are honoring her.

You might even want to suggest that children be prepared to put a specified number of articles into each box, so that your child does not feel like he has to defend everything on his turf. Teaching your child to declutter does not have to be traumatic, if you playfully point out to your child some alternatives to do with items. Sometimes it is helpful to have a box and ask the child to place in it things they do not want to throw away but have no space for in their room. Take the box, store it in the garage or other storage, and agree to look at it again in six months. Chances are your child will be willing to release the items in six months because he would have forgotten about them.

Children will release items more easily if they are being given away to a good cause. Our kids are more altruistic than you might think. If a child knows something is being given to an individual he will part with it more easily. A friend, whose daughter is a sliver taller than my daughter, gets her daughter to part with special clothes by asking her to give them to my daughter. We have donated to many charities. I always try to give my kids a face to put to the recipient. For instance, once we were donating toys to a special needs children's ministry; we read books about special needs and I showed my daughters the organization's pamphlet. They felt good about giving their things away.

Another way to get your child to release clutter is to have her create a memory box. Each of my children has a memory box to store in their room or at times the basement. My kids tend to want to save papers, letters, birthday cards, doll dresses, old audio books, die-cast racing cars and a multitude of crafts. By asking them to limit their collections as opposed to throwing them away I get much more cooperation. Remember it may be junk to you but it is your child's cherished possessions. Your relationship with your child is more important than a clean room. It is easy to fall into the trap of making a clean room a power struggle. Be willing to bend and allow your child to keep some items you may consider clutter as long as it is not a health issue.

After you have decluttered, move to step two. Divide the room into four quadrants or activity zones. These zones will mark where activities take place in the room. Of course, the quadrants will not be exactly equal because some rooms may be less regular in shape than others or have obstructions that prevent the room from being divided equally. Next choose the four major activities that take place in the room. It might be playing with toys, reading area, homework area, entertainment (that's television and music), and sleeping. One or two activities may be combined within a quadrant.

You can determine what the quadrants should be by observing or asking your child what they do in their room. If you find they are doing too much in their room you may want to eliminate some activities. When my children were preschoolers I did not allow toys in the room because I was generally the one cleaning up; we eliminated playing in their room so I would not have to be responsible for picking up toys. As they got older and more responsible, I released them to do other activities in their rooms including playing.

You may recall you should always be specific with your child. Tell her to go upstairs and pick up all the clothes, toys, papers, books and collectibles off the floor. It works best if you instruct the child to go and pick up all the clothes first. Watch her put the soiled clothes in the laundry and place the fresh clothes in the dresser drawers. I am constantly surprised at the amount of clean laundry in a child's room that just never made it into their bureau after washday simply because it got mixed in with the dirty laundry again. One way to eliminate this problem is to offer coupons with expiration dates for prizes for clothes that are put away immediately. The child has to unload all her clean clothes from the laundry basket to find the coupon for a prize. An expiration date ensures the task is done quickly. Your child only has to miss the expiration date of one coupon to be motivated to put her laundry away in a timely fashion.

After each task is completed tell the child to move on to the next task such as picking up toys. Once she puts the toys in their proper space then move on to the next item. By doing it like this, slowly and sequentially, your child is not overwhelmed and can easily comprehend what you are requiring of him. Your ADD child may need to come back to you after she picks up all the books and you may need to further subdivide the task by telling her to sort the books into categories such as school, library or family books. Commend your child for each step or sub-step in the process. After each item is placed where it belongs, encourage your child to make certain everything is in its right quadrant. For example, bedding should not be in the homework quadrant. For young children you may initially need to label the quadrants or add pictorial cues for them. Older children who create their own systems will be motivated simply because it is their own choosing. You may want to make certain they put cleaning time in their calendar.

The best time to organize your children's clothing is on laundry day. Generally the clothes they want to wear and care about are in the laundry and it will be easier to sort through the remaining items. I used to keep a box by the washing machine and when I did the laundry and I noticed an item was too small I put it in the give-away box, which was promptly dumped into a bag to be given away. I handed down my daughters' clothing from one to the other by having a seasonal box of clothes that did not fit. I used file boxes and labeled them clearly before I stacked them in the basement. You can line the boxes with plastic garage bags. I once heard from a mom that she places a piece of a fresh stick of peppermint gum still in its wrapper to keep the clothes smelling fresh and the bugs out.

I use file boxes to file many items. I label the boxes with a letter and number then record the contents in my PDA (personal digital assistant). For instance, I might write A-1 for a mother's memory box then list everything I have in the box in my PDA. Storage space is a major issue in growing families. Consider all your options for increasing storage space before you move or do a major home renovation. Perhaps you can store stuff under items in your home. You can purchase elevating bed coasters that allow for higher storage under the bed. You can also use these coasters for certain types of sofas.

Look for creative ways to store things. Do not think in the typical way. Hanging shoe bags are excellent for storing small toys, scarves or many different kinds of children's accessories and objects. You can also store things from the ceiling. Hanging plant holders in the kitchen can store weighty fruit or other heavy items. Think very nontraditionally. Store items on doors, in drawers and almost any place you find room.

As much as possible handle everything only once. This includes mail, soiled socks, homework and notes—just about anything. Make decisions on these items quickly. Indecision is the cause of much mess. Organize things at point of use. If you like to read in your easy chair in the evening, make sure a bookshelf or basket is located nearby. Utilize multiple items when necessary. For instance, make more than one changing station for the baby if necessary: one upstairs and downstairs. Ask yourself what works for your family.

Eventually your child will have to move to self-management. The next chapter is perhaps the most important because your child must successfully deal with his weaknesses in order to become strong.

FURTHER TIPS

- For younger children's artwork and papers, consider creating a Weekly Wall of Fame on a bulletin board in their room or study areas. Every week or so, tack up some of the work they bring home from school. Papers can then be sorted to what needs to be filed and what can safely be tossed.

- Work out a "clean plan," creating an actual map of where things go. Place collectibles, trophies, stuffed animals, doll accessories, CDs, pens and pencils and the laundry basket on the map. Tape the map on the inside of a closet door so your child can refer to it often.

- Work out a reward plan. For a month of cleaning, add a little extra allowance or buy your preteen a treat or a music CD or DVD.

- Encourage your child to throw out the unused, un-wanted and unloved items in his room. Encourage him, but do not throw away or discard anything without his approval.

- When you absolutely can't stand it anymore, make your child's favorite dessert, then tell her she is welcome to have some once her room is clean.

8 Moving to Self-Management

No one will say it, but probably every parent's worst fear about their ADD child is that he will never be fully self-sufficient. It looms over parents' heads like a bad omen and it is revisited each time a shoe is lost, homework is misplaced, or an emotional meltdown occurs. The thought plagues us: Will he ever be able to live on his own?

ADD children have many strengths including vivid creativity and the ability to focus on a problem until they arrive at a solution. Like us, our children must also be aware of their weaknesses and plan for the inevitably of the reoccurrence of some typical problems including time management and organization. They need to be aware of times of transitions, relentlessly use their planners, and engage in practical ways to help keep themselves on track.

Overall children have little concept of time. ADD children have two major time management issues. One that we briefly discussed in Chapter 5 is the issue of making transitions. Transitioning, moving from one activity to another and refocusing on the new activity, is a difficult skill to master. When moving from one activity/environment to the other, our minds are generally occupied with the movement and the scattered attention of the old and new and we get caught in the moment. In times of transition, we tend to misplace our keys or forget what we went upstairs for. The change in environment causes us to get lost in the moment.

Children who get lost in the moment find it extremely difficult to transition from one activity to the other. ADD children have the greatest problems with transitions because they lose focus so easily. In fact, you probably noticed that your child tends to forget his schoolbooks or assignments during transitional times at school. The child has to recognize transitional times. In early elementary, good teachers are adept at readying children for transitional times. They will flash the classroom lights or use a hand signal and children recognize a change is coming. As suggested previously, you can use music or singing to transition your child to a new activity. But, what happens when you cannot be there to provide those transitional cues?

ADD children have to learn to look objectively at their schedule and determine their own transitional times such as leaving school and remembering books, moving from one environment to the next, etc. These times should be noted in their planners and they will need to seek help on ways to remember items and to maintain focus during transitional times.

ADD children are also known to hyper-focus. They can get so caught up in an activity that the passing of time evades them, especially when doing an enjoyable activity. Hyper-focusing has its benefits but the child still needs to be aware of when she has a propensity to hyper-focus. Timers, especially visual timers, work best because they help your child see time passing. Children should work on creative or high intensity projects with timers to prevent hyper-focusing.

Daily planners are a necessity. ADD children tend to be global learners in that they need to see how all the parts fit together. I realize this is an over-generalization but I have found when working with ADD children that the light bulb seems to go on when they can see their whole schedule laid out for them. Planners are essential for them. The calendar is an essential tool that helps your child manage himself. He can plan for his transitions in his planner. Remember to help your child use his planner and adapt it to his needs. Many schools give out calendars but within a few weeks none of the students are using them because no one ever took the time to show them how to use it and to reinforce its use over time. Your ADD child needs training in how to use his calendar/planner.

A planner should be easy to use and not visually distracting. Older children can write their own to-do lists, but they will still need help from you. They may be prone to think idealistically and I have noticed many children abandon their planners because they over-plan and therefore theorize that the planner/organizer does not work. Nothing could be further from the truth. To help your child, encourage her to put time estimates near every to-do item in her planner. For instance your child might put "homework (45 minutes)" as an entry. Using a planner helps your child to get a full visual presentation of her schedule.

A planner/organizer, whether digital or paper, is a vital tool for teaching a child to manage deadlines, a school workload, social activities and home commitments. Seeing time in context helps one to think realistically about planning. I generally encourage parents to make a master calendar for their child that includes homework and study time. Homework and study time need to be distinguished from one another. Remember the planner you choose for your child should have the capacity to see a week-at-a-glance so it should be easy to list more than one event or deadline in the allotted date boxes. This is important when teaching your child to plan study time. I have actually used teacher planner books for some of my clients because they allow the youngster to see the week in totality and include enough space to post after-school and home commitments.

While many students are enjoying using electronic planners, I am conservative in that I still strongly advocate ADD/

ADHD students primarily have hardcopy calendars until they are solidified in planning and contextual time management skills, because electronic instruments rarely show a full week at a glance with all the commitments clearly documented. For instance, on my PDA an asterisk indicates I have a scheduled event on a specified day but it does not tell me what kind of commitment it is or help in my planning. Inevitably, I find my PDA to be an organizing not planning tool. Incidentally, if your child sees you using a planner he will often begin to imitate you.

When your child gets her planner, encourage her to post all her time commitments in it, then review the schedule. Did she include basketball practices? Rehearsal for the school play? Volunteer time at the local hospital? Time to walk the dog she begged you to get for her? The visual presentation helps her to be more practical when planning. Eventually older children understand once a time slot is filled, nothing else can fit into their schedule. It takes time. It is a good idea to create a master schedule with your child that includes a definite bed and wake-up time because children will tend to want to use up all their time without consequence and in the process run their bodies down.

ADD children also need preparation time in their schedules every day. They should be preparing for the next day's activities. It is not enough for your child to schedule homework time. He must also put time in his schedule for getting ready for school the next day. Scheduled preparation time is a necessity for ADD children. This is a skill they must acclimate themselves to such that they practice it well into adulthood.

Remembering will generally be a challenge for ADD children. It is therefore important they integrate school, home and extracurricular commitments all in one planner. Once this is achieved, the child will be able to plan his own time realistically and formulate a realistic schedule that uses preparation time. Most importantly, your child should be able to look at his planner and identify his transitional times. He might find that when leaving school he wants to make a checklist, one with visual cues much like the schedule checklist from Chapter 5.

Middle-school students (ages 10–14) really need help in this area because elementary teachers for the most part will help students to make transitions by allotting time daily for students to gather all their materials for homework. This is not to suggest ADD students do poorly in middle school. On the contrary, many will thrive better because they get to move around more and have a frequent change in their environment. It does mean they have to remember more often because they make so many transitions.

Finally, the ADD child has to know how to stay on track. One way that is very effective is to encourage the child to say aloud to himself what he is doing so that he is not distracted. For instance, when getting ready for school after he has verified that he has done everything on his morning checklist he might say as he is coming down the stairs, "I am going to get my backpack." He can repeat this a few times to avoid being distracted by the television or computer. He should say what he is doing in the affirmative. This does not work in school or other social settings but he can mutter it quietly to himself especially during transitions.

Some say the scent of peppermint and lemon helps them concentrate. If possible, allow your child to sniff or suck on peppermint before starting a homework assignment. Some teachers report that applying Velcro to a student's desk keeps the student calm and able to focus by occasionally stroking the affixed Velcro. Different textures, while disturbing to some children, are soothing to others. Your child may have to experiment with various scents and textures. Deep and timed breathing also helps calm us. Your child may have to learn to breathe deeply from the diaphragm before an exam or at times when he needs to concentrate. When we are relaxed, we think more clearly.

Boredom is another issue ADD children will have to learn to manage. According to Blake Taylor, who authored *ADHD and Me* as an ADHD teenager, his impulsivity was generally triggered by boredom. Encourage your child to be involved in structured sports or other activities. Boredom is a symptom they can recognize and deal with before their impulsivity gets them into trouble. I suggest parents have bins with lids of art projects, model and construction kits for these inevitable times of boredom. Boredom can also be offset by careful planning. Even planning free time to sit and think reduces times of impulsivity because the child has a planned activity even if that activity is to sit still.

Children also need to increase their frustration threshold. ADD children are notorious for being impatient and at times obnoxious (depending on the type of ADD). To raise your child's frustration threshold, use a timer and gradually require her to wait longer for gratification. This is not to punish the child but to help her see she can wait longer than she thinks she is able to. Encourage older children to set goals to wait longer. Use timers and lavish your children with praise. Older children may need to set their own goals and provide a reward for themselves when they achieve a goal. This is a life skill they can develop early.

ADD children will have to be honest with themselves and recognize their weaknesses. Contrary to popular myths, ADD is not outgrown. ADD adults simply learn how to manage their ADD tendencies of distraction, forgetfulness and disorganization. They may recognize the propensity to be distracted and write everything down and then place those reminders in prominent places where they are least likely to be forgotten. They may rely on electronic reminders or other systems.

Accountability may also mean our children turn to ADD coaches, professional organizers, friends and family when they are overwhelmed. Sometimes ADD children need to be aware of their weaknesses as they build on their strengths. Your child will need to know it is not a weakness to reach out to others for assistance. In fact, the strong man is aware of his weaknesses. You may want to connect your child with support groups and organizations that will help them. (See the list of useful resources.)

FURTHER TIPS

- If you prefer, you can place your checklist in a three-ring binder instead of on the wall as long as it is accessible to both you and your children. Checklists will need to be updated as children get older.

- Label everything! Use a computer printer to make simple graphic labels for young children. Pictures of socks, shirts, dolls or blocks help remind the child where these items belong. Enhance reading skills for older children by using large-type word labels. Slap labels everywhere: inside and outside of drawers, on shelf edges and on the plastic shoebox storage containers that belong there, on boxes and bookcases and filing cubes. Playing "match the label" can be fun—and turns toy pickup into a game.

- Build a maintenance routine. Otherwise, children will be easily frustrated. Their room is clean, they play and, suddenly, their room is back to messy normal. Help children stop the cycle by building maintenance routines into the family's day. "Morning Pickup" straightens the comforter/blanket, returns the pillow to the bed, and gets yesterday's clothing to the laundry hamper. "Evening Pickup" precedes dressing for bed, and involves putting away the day's toys.

- Take a child's eye view. Get down to your child's eye level to help her get organized. Look at your child's space, storage, furniture and possessions from her vantage point. The view may surprise you!

9 Managing Your Home

Many parents confess that while they want to organize their children they too struggle with organization themselves. Before you can effectively manage others, you must first manage yourself. You might consider this chapter a quick organizing review for yourself. There are some simple rules.

Start with "I will put away everything I take out." Most household messes result from people simply not putting items back where they belong. For instance, when you use the hammer, put it back in the toolbox immediately after use.

Make certain that you know the purpose of each area in your home so that you can communicate it to others. In my organizing workshops I usually take the mothers through an exercise where they determine the purpose of each room in their home by determining what activities occur in that particular room. In a nutshell, I encourage them to view each room in their house as a part of a greater whole.

You can efficiently keep your home clean if kids are paying attention to how each room is used. Just like how you set up zones in your kids' bedrooms you can set up rooms in your home to reflect the purpose of the room. Once you have determined the purpose of each room in your home, make sure that you use it for that purpose. Open your mail at the designated spot, not at the door or the mailbox or any other place at your home. It does take time. For complete information on this process, get free download sheets and instructions from my website www.momtime.net.

There are a few other principles you may use as well. As much as possible, handle everything only once. This includes clothes, mail, hobby items, etc. This is a big time saver because if you are handling items more than once it generally means you have no specific place or home for the item. You can encourage your children to put items back in their home, which basically means put things back where they belong. Keep things where you are most likely to use them.

The standard rule for home organization is that things should be stored conveniently where a bit of effort is used to retrieve something but no effort is used to put it back. If you are using scissors, they might be stored in the bottom of a box. You may have to expend some effort to get to them but since you need them that will not matter to you. It will then be very easy for you to put the scissors back in the box. This means fewer out of place items. As I have been pointing out throughout this book it is imperative that cleaning schedules are posted. You will get more cooperation if the rules are clear, concise and posted. At times you also may need to adjust your personal standard of order and cleanliness. If you tend to be messy, you need to raise your standard. If you are too meticulous, you may need to lower it so that your home does not become an antiseptic hospital.

Your home should be a home of love, not law. You set the mood of your home; therefore, you should always have your own calendar book and regularly review the purpose of your home. It will change as your family changes. Go with the flow. Schedule time for you. It takes time to change. A new habit is firmly established after 21 days, so be patient with your family and yourself. It is all worth it. The ultimate action plan for change in your home starts with you. Genuine change occurs internally and takes time. The most important part of your home is unseen by the human eye, but felt deeply by the human heart. It is the atmosphere of your home. Atmosphere is reflected in the way you keep order in your home. You can keep order by love or by law. When you keep order by law, your home is regimented. Family members keep order out of fear of angry reprisals. Mistakes are not tolerated. There are a lot of rules and regulations to keep everyone in line and the house showroom perfect. Rules are made to restrict. There is a strong authoritarian spirit in this kind of home. The home is clean, yet antiseptic. In short, this home is clean, sterile and cold!

On the other hand, when you keep order by love, your home is orderly, friendly and very comfortable. Most things are in place, with an occasional mess here and there. The rules and regulations are there to maintain the peace. The rules are based on collective understanding and are viewed as a means of protection for everyone. Family members' mistakes are not met with angry reprisals, but as opportunities to grow more responsible. A strong sense of team spirit is felt. This home is neat and comfortable. It is warm and endearing. Ultimately, the essential atmosphere in your home governs the physical atmosphere. Our homes can be either very legalistic, ruled by law and enforced by anger and punishment, or it can be ordered by love enforced by compassion. You can set the atmosphere of your home. The decision is up to you. Do not let your struggles to keep the house in order hinder your relationship with your child.

Managing a household involves an understanding of two key elements: inventory and maintenance. Everything we do falls into one of these categories. Inventory items keep the family moving and spontaneous. These items are their needs. Most times these things cannot be delayed. They include food, clean clothes, etc. I have to feed my children. They need to wear clean clothes. I have to pay the electricity bill, because I need lights.

Maintenance items can be delayed. The kitchen floor may be sticky, but the family will still function. Your windows may be full of grime, but you can still see out of them. I don't advocate sticky floors or grimy windows but I hope you get my point. Inventory items should be taken care of first in your home. This will free you to address maintenance issues.

One important inventory item is the laundry. This is a job with various steps. Often we neglect to think through the whole process; therefore, we do not complete the laundry in a one-time segment. Reduce the steps you take when doing laundry and you'll see what I mean. I hate doing laundry therefore I do it every day. No, it's not some redemptive character building spiritual exercise. I simply hate dealing with the volume of laundry so I try to do it every day so it doesn't pile up. With a husband who goes to the gym daily and three active kids this is actually quite easy for me. Also, get help from others. Train little ones to do easy elements of a task, such as simply sorting the laundry, with older ones helping with the more complex parts of the chore. Teenagers should definitely be doing their own laundry. My kids have their own laundry baskets, so they fold and put away their own clothes. We have had only one flood in the basement when the kids wanted to surprise me for Mother's Day by doing the laundry.

The other area in the home that is of major concern is meal preparation. This too is a multi-faceted task. It involves shopping, planning, preparing and cooking. The time spent in this area also can be reduced. You should only be going to the grocery store once a week or less. This can surely be accomplished with some planning. First, visit the store you frequent the most and write down the items in each aisle. Next, type it up, if possible. Photocopy it. Write your grocery list on it; it will reduce your shopping time. You can post the paper in the kitchen so that when you notice you are low on an item you can simply write it on the list. This will keep you from running out of items and from going to the store so frequently. It also speeds up the time when you are in the store. You should also write out a tentative menu for a week and go shopping for these items at one time. For working parents, there are so many great cookbooks with simple meals that do not take long to prepare.

Take time every Saturday to plan the next week's meals. I try to plan for two weeks' worth of meals. Do not forget the kids' snacks and lunch foods. You can also cook double portions when you cook and freeze the second portion. You can also cook for two weeks, or even a month at a time, if you have the freezer space. Usually I purchase prepared foods when they go on sale. This helps at times.

As I share in my home management workshops, managing the mail saved my marriage...only joking! Seriously though, every family should have a paper management plan. You can get inexpensive colored folders from an office supply store or supermarket. They often go on sale right after Christmas, which is usually when I replace my worn folders. Every piece of mail should be placed immediately in one of the following folders, or tossed in the trash! Label your folders as follows:

- Red: To Pay—Your fiscal folder holds all your bills which need to be paid. A calendar should be placed inside the folder so that you can see when a particular bill is due.

- White: To Do—This action folder contains those things upon which you will take immediate action.

- Yellow: To Hold—This pending folder is to put things on hold; you will eventually use them but they do not need to be filed away. These include wedding invitations, directions, trash schedules, etc.

- Green: To File—This filing folder is for all those items that should be filed away at a later date in your household file cabinet.

- Blue: Partner—The partner folder is for correspondence relating to your partner. Now the mail is in one uniform spot for him to read.

- Orange: To Read—The reading folder is for any mail that will take over ten minutes to read.

Another area of home management involves scheduling and time management. A family calendar is a necessity; list kids' scouting meetings, recitals, plays, trips, etc. Put down your commitments too.

Everyone should use the family calendar. You can refer to it before you make a commitment. It also helps to slow down the pace of the family a bit. You can put in the family meetings and special dinners, etc., you want all of the family to attend. Calendars are great! You should also have your own personal calendar and make appointments with yourself. These appointments can be for personal development, spiritual growth, etc. Either way, post them so family members will know you are unavailable at these times. You need to make the time to fill yourself up before you pour into others. Mothers, particularly, spend much time pouring into the lives of others, yet very little time filling themselves back up.

You can also reduce a lot of stress by having a family bulletin board/communication center. I have one in the kitchen. You can use a horizontal file folder or cover a cereal box with contact paper. Train your children to put notes in the box. This way you can read them at your leisure and not when you are cooking dinner, or otherwise occupied. The communication center can also be used to place encouraging notes to other family members. You can also have a suggestion box. The suggestion box can be used for kids and adults to write down their ideas about how the family can effectively function. A calendar should be near the family communication center.

These are just a few ideas that can help you to run your family more efficiently. Household management involves developing good habits and remember: a habit is something you do without thinking. Good thinking forms good habits. We set the standard for our households with our habits. It is not so important that our homes are spick and span clean but that we are constantly working to improve our home management skills to serve our families.

Establish house rules and cleaning schedules and post them. You will get more cooperation if the rules are clear, concise and posted! If you tend to be messy, you need to raise your standard. If you are too meticulous, you may need to alter it so that your home does not become an antiseptic hospital. Assess your storage needs before you go and buy organization products. Too often people see sales on organizing products and buy them only to realize they will not work for them because they do not address the issues that caused disorder. For instance, I once went to a friend's home office to help her organize it. She complained that she did not have any desk space because her desk was so small. Yet she had many desk organizers that were taking up room. When I suggested she get vertical organizers and use her wall space a light bulb went on. She had never considered that keeping the desk completely clear would spur her productivity.

Think of creative ways to deal with clutter so that you are not exerting a lot of mental, physical or emotional energy on little things that really do not matter. As I mentioned earlier, the lost and found box was initially implemented simply because I did not like reminding the kids to pick up their stuff. Anything left out of place was put into the lost and found box. I did not nag or complain. I simply placed it in the box. The kids had to pay money to retrieve their belonging from the box.

FURTHER TIPS

- Try to improve the physical appearance of every room you enter or leave in your home. The kids can really have fun with this one!

- Simplify everything in your home. Follow the basics of good home management. Always try to do more than one thing at a time. Cut down on clutter. Have a book sale or book swap with other parents. Sell or trade books your children have outgrown.

- Get cotton matching clothes that require little ironing. Children's clothes with bright designs on them hide stains. Avoid conflicts by allowing your child to choose which clothes he wants to wear the night before school. Even if your child's school does not have a uniform, you can decide on a personal school uniform for your child. It may simply be jeans and a sweat shirt, which is economical and easy.

- Invest in the right cleaning products and tools to keep your home in order and the family operating smoothly. Use a squeegee to clean windows and bathroom tiles. Use disinfectant wipes in the bathroom. Encourage family members (especially little boys) to use them to wipe the toilet and sink after bathroom use.

10 ADD/ADHD Questions

Question
It seems I am always repeating myself to my child. Will he ever get it?

Answer
It can be frustrating to repeat oneself but we can learn to say the same thing differently. For instance, I like to whisper audible instructions to many of my ADD clients. They stop and really focus in on a whisper. Nonverbal cues also are effective. You can simply tap your child's shoulder or point to a visual reminder. You may also use charts or checklists. If you have your family schedule posted and your son is chatting with his little brother in the kitchen instead of sitting at the table and doing homework you can point to the chart indicating it is homework time. It is important when getting your child back on task that you do not engage in long conversations with him. Both of you will get off track arguing about how he was only talking to his little brother for one minute, or you'll get the "You don't trust me" soliloquy every parent dreads. It does not matter how the conversation turns out; you lose because your child will have sidetracked you

from the issue at hand. So music, singing, touch, charts and other objects help us to repeat ourselves without words.

Question
How can I get my child's attention?

Answer
Be sure your son makes eye contact with you and can repeat what you have said to him in his own words. He should not just parrot you. Give your child directions one at a time in short declarative sentences. For instance, you might say, "Turn off the television and come to me." After the child has come to you then give the next action you want him to take. Use simple declarative sentences with an action verb so the child knows what he should do.

Question
I understand my child should use his planner for transitional times but I don't quite understand how this can be practical.

Answer
Ultimately, your child learns to plan for transitions herself. For instance, I worked with a family that used to pay library fines a lot until I told the children to record their list of checked out library books in their planners as soon as they got home from the library. The parents had to remind them but gradually they began to internalize the process. This shift was aided by the children paying for their own lost library books. Eventually they got the point. As parents, it's important to note that at times we will sound like the proverbial broken record until our children grasp a concept. The planner helps them to get the point themselves.

Question
How can I get my child to sit still for our worship service?

Answer
ADD children tend to like textures. One teacher I knew actually glued Velcro to the underside of the desk of some of her wandering students to encourage them to remain in their seats. Masking tape and other quiet finger toys or toys with movable parts are good for little ones.

Question
Are temper tantrums solely time related?

Answer
Temper tantrums reflect your child's low frustration threshold and an inability to understand time. You can avoid a lot of temper tantrums if you distract your child from his current activity with a promise of another exciting activity. Engage in purposeful distraction. Choose something the child wants to do and offer that as a worthy alternative. For instance, when you are at the park and your child does not want to go home suggest a fun activity like watching a favorite videotape or a coloring activity. It is senseless to reason with a child having a tantrum because at that point he has lost control and definitely is not in a state of mind to be rational. In addition, an adult's concerns about making dinner or picking up a sibling make no sense to a self-centered absorbed child. Instead, approach your child enthusiastically and say, "Let's go home and watch *Arthur*" (my favorite PBS kids' show).

Question
It seems like I'm planning for my child all day such that we don't have time for fun or spontaneity. Is this what ADD parenting is all about?

Answer

No, we don't want to rob our children of the joy of childhood but if we do not plan for times of transition or times when our children will be overly aroused emotionally or physically then we can be blindsided. We should always plan with a bit of flexibility in mind. When making your child's schedule, be careful not to overwhelm your child with too many activities. Give broad and basic information so that the schedule sheet is not too cluttered. Children with processing problems cannot easily take in information if it is too visually distracting, thus while you want your schedule sheet to be aesthetically pleasing you also want to keep it as bare bones as possible.

Question

At what point should I stop helping my child to get up in the morning?

Answer

It depends on the child but the sooner the child can take the responsibility for waking the better he will feel about himself, especially tweens and teens.

Question

How can I recognize and plan transitions for my child?

Answer

Planning transitions simply means getting your child to anticipate change. Your child should know her schedule. Post the schedule throughout your home. Put it in the kitchen, bathroom and your child's room. You can also laminate it and place it in inconspicuous places throughout your home such as underneath a book or in a magazine rack to protect your child's privacy. Some children do not like visitors to know what they perceive as "their personal business." Add pictures from old magazines or other universal symbols that are easily drawn, like a fork and a spoon for mealtimes and a bed for naptime. Children tend to be very visual and it will permeate their memory if they can see it visually. This is especially effective if you put the schedule in many places and laminate it so the child can not only see it but handle it as well. This provides real multi-sensory input.

Question
Why is a calendar so important especially if my child doesn't even look at it?

Answer
A basic family calendar posted in a prominent place in the home is essential. As children wait excitedly for an event you can reinforce the fact that time is measured in seconds, minutes, hours and days. You should refer to the calendar and place important dates on it so that your child will want to look at it. Do not underestimate the power of a prominently displayed family calendar because your child will associate days or time with something tangible. It is a general rule when working with your child always to provide concrete examples for abstract terms. Remember also that a child has a nonlinear concept of time; this view of time hinders her ability to wait. It can be irritating for us to say over and over again we are not there yet but it is equally frustrating for the child caught in monotony and unable to see or feel time passing.

Question
How can I get my child to learn to wait?

Answer
All children live in the immediate or now. To help your child transition to an understanding of time give him something to do while he is waiting. For instance, when waiting to go

to Grandma's house have your child cross off the days on the calendar and perhaps make a craft for Grandma that might take five days to complete. The completion date should coincide with the scheduled visit to Grandma. When in the car, he can even count landmarks until you arrive at your destination. This will not likely occupy him the whole time so it is best for you to have a car bag with toys to entertain him on long trips.

Question
Your systems sound great but what happens when my child loses his notebook?

Answer
Actually, I prefer a child not to carry all his papers to school. A binder and a paper filing system helps your child leave many papers at home. If your child insists on using a spiral notebook, get one with the least amount of paper.

Question
Do you have any suggestions for my daughter who physically cannot regularly carry a heavy binder?

Answer
Yes. She could file all her pages at home in her binder. She simply needs a pad of three-hole paper to take notes. I would also suggest you get an accordion folder and label the sections for each class so that she can at least file her school papers immediately or have a place she can place and retrieve teacher handouts, exams, etc., until she can file them at home.

Question
My daughter is doing everything on the computer. She is overwhelmed and I am really baffled how to help her. What should I do?

Answer

Relax, it is really not as bad as you think it is. On your desktop create a folder for your child and within that folder create a folder for each subject. As with regular paper, most items can be deleted or trashed when the marking period is over or if your child will be taking a cumulative subject test or standardized exam; there is no need to refer back to material that the child has already been tested on. This information can easily be accessed for future use on the internet, through library books, etc. Old quizzes and tests can be used as study aids.

Question

My 15-year-old daughter resists me helping her organize her backpack. What can I do?

Answer

She may be worried about you finding her private papers or perhaps failed tests. Ask her to sort the papers first herself, taking out anything she does not want you to see. After she has removed these papers, she may be more accepting of your assistance. Also, share with her the different ways that you may be able to help her after reading this book. You might also want to promise her you will remain calm when working with her. She may assume the whole experience is going to result in the two of you arguing. It might help to approach her with a signed contract that you promise not to get upset no matter what the backpack looks like and you further agree not to lecture her on proper paper management. If none of that works, give her an ultimatum or date to have the backpack cleaned out herself.

Question

How do I begin to sort through all the junk from my son's locker?

Answer
You begin by separating the contents into categories: text-books, clothing, CDs, notebooks, loose papers, etc., then decide with your son what items can be thrown out. You will need a lot of floor space to sort through everything and you might want to create the categories before you just dump all the contents of his canvas bag. Do not sort through everything at home then throw it back in the same bag. Separate it into categories and put it in heavy duty large freezer bags. Identify on your sketched locker map exactly where items will be placed so your son can easily place them in his locker. Locker shelves are also helpful to keep items organized. (See the list of useful resources.)

Question
Even after I spend time helping my daughter clean out her backpack, by the end of the year, it's a mess. Any suggestions?

Answer
You need to establish a weekly time when she cleans her backpack out at home. Any new routine needs lots of follow-up and reward for its implementation.

Question
I see my nine-year-old daughter doing her homework but she is not turning it in at school. She puts it in a folder. What can I do?

Answer
Your child needs more than just a folder for school; she needs a system. Is the folder easily accessible when she gets to school? Be careful not to overcomplicate the organizing process. Some parents give their children so many different colored folders that the child does not know from which folder to retrieve information. Keep the system simple. One homework folder is sufficient for elementary students (ages 5–10).

Question

My child cannot seem to complete his laundry the same time as he cleans his room. His brother also has ADD and is able to do both. What should I do?

Answer

ADD affects different individuals in different ways, even siblings. For the most part, an ADD child should only do one job/project at a time. It might help if you broke up laundry into distinct tasks. For instance, sorting the laundry would be one step and considered a task. Assign that task and once he completes that task move on to the next task.

Question

My ADD child gets caught up designing a robot with his K'NEX building blocks and gets angry when I stop him. He is doing a wonderful job with the K'NEX but every day it is the same thing: he tantrums when it is time to stop. I feel guilty making him stop something he loves but the tantrums are horrible.

Answer

ADD children also have the tendency to hyper-focus. We all have experienced working hard on a creative project and getting so caught up in it that we lose track of time. Writers call it being in the flow. A timer may initially help by giving him a specified time for designing with his K'NEX blocks. Some ADD children are prone to get so caught up in the small details of a project that they do not see the big picture.

Question

How do you deal with temper tantrums?

Answer

A preschooler typically has a tantrum because he is frustrated. They simply don't understand the concept of time and delayed reward and it's just an excess of emotions. For instance, if you are going to the park with your child then follow these steps.

1. Engage the child before you leave. To engage the child make eye contact and tell him what you expect of him at the park. Give him a short list of what you are going to do at the park. If you have a visual aid or an actual photograph this will also be useful in helping your child understand the sequence of events at the park. Tell him that when it is time to leave the park, he will put on his sandals and get out of the sandbox (assuming the sandbox is the last part of the sequence).

2. Once at the park remind him of the sequence and emphasize that putting his sandals back on and getting out the sandbox is the cue it is time to leave the park. If you have your visual aid show it to him to reinforce the park exit process. This also helps him to understand time. Your child should repeat the simple sequence back to you using his fingers to denote each new activity.

3. When it is time to leave the park, give him four timed warnings with accompanying instructions or preparations to go home. These should occur approximately at ten minutes, five minutes, three minutes, one minute. Finally, tell him it is time to put on his sandals and pack his toys in his duffle bag. It is a good idea to give him something else to do such as pick up the diaper bag or pack a bag of toys to distract him from focusing on leaving the park. If you have a great voice (and do not mind if other mothers hear you) you could also sing a silly "it's time to go" song especially if you sing the song at home. Some parents find exit songs help a child to move faster and accept the fact that he is changing environments. You will find following this progression will lessen the occurrence of emotional upheavals.

Question

My child likes the fresh air and likes to do his homework with his back to the window but it seems he is easily distracted by cars, barking dogs, etc. Any suggestions?

Answer

You could get earplugs. (See the list of useful resources.) You might also try using a noise machine with sounds of ocean waves or birds chirping, or play light classical music. The steady background music may help him ignore the other noises. Or he simply may not be able to sit by the window when actually doing his homework but may be able to look out the window during timed homework breaks.

Question

How can I get all my children excited about being trained in household chores since it is not a fun process?

Answer

Speak to your children about the team process. It is imperative we give all children the opportunity to serve and be successful and part of a team. A sense of belonging is a primal need of all children and they will quickly grasp the team concept if you present it to them. They inherently understand that being part of a family or a team requires everyone to pull their own weight. Siblings of ADD children often resent the fact that parents require little or nothing from their brother or sister. This leads to sibling resentment, which feeds sibling rivalry, which creates an atmosphere of stress in the home. We can reduce a lot of family stress just by everyone sharing the load.

Question

I have ADD myself and I find it difficult to organize myself. How can I help my children?

Answer

Generally, you have the advantage of understanding how your child feels. A great book I would suggest is *ADD Friendly Ways to Organize Your Life* by Judith Kolberg and Kathleen Nadeau. You may find some principles that work for your child will also work for you. In particular, the principles of posting your schedule and using color help, as well as highlighting your planner. There are also many tools available and Internet websites specifically geared to adults. Adults with ADD generally find working alongside someone else keeps them on track. For instance, you may have a friend help you clean out your closet. Visit www.add123.org for tips for ADD parents.

11 Helpful Tips

The following are ideas that have worked for parents with ADD/ADHD children. It is not necessary to read through the whole list in one go, but keep it handy. Often parents of ADD/ADHD children will reach a point of saturation when working with their children if what once worked no longer seems to yield the same results. At the saturation point you will need to try something new, and this list will prove to be quite a valuable resource.

CHORES

- Make placing a star, check mark or some indication of completion on their chore chart the child's responsibility. Your child will enjoy looking at the accumulated star evidence of her accomplishment.

- Make certain your child has the same clean-up routine daily. While it is true many children enjoy rotating the chores, many ADD/ADHD children and teenagers thrive in predictability and structure.

- Do not rush your ADD child to complete a chore in the same time as you would another child; give him time to process information. Add a bit of time to any task you give him to complete. Let him know it is a game to see how completely he does a task, not how fast he completes a task.

- While your ADD/ADHD child likes structure, she also likes to have choices. So make cleaning a game. Allow her to choose different products and record her task completion time. She works best when she can race against herself day to day.

- Post a colorful sign at home with "Stop, Think and Act" so your child can learn better impulse control. Before he does anything have him stop, think and then act to do the chore.

- Your child will do better with assigned chores that are short in duration so try to get his assigned chores down to a few minutes. You can add more chores as he perfects the shorter ones.

- When it is necessary to repeat yourself to your child, say it in a different way. You can sometimes play the whisper game where you whisper loudly the instructions. Your child will focus in on a whisper.

- Do not rush your child to complete a chore. Never compare siblings or say things like "Your brother made up his bed in only seven minutes; why is it taking you fifteen?" It is also a good idea to reward your child when he completes a task with minimal verbal or tactile reminders.

- Use nonverbal reminders to get kids to help out. This allows the child to correct her own behavior and to feel good about herself.

- Play "beat the clock" with your child. Try to speed up mundane or routine activities.

- Write notes to your child asking him to do specified chores. He will like getting the note and perceive the chores as positive since it relates to you.

DRESSING

- Put matching kids' outfits together so kids can dress themselves. This is especially important in the event of a midday clothing change.

- Use a mesh bag to keep up with socks and other small items. Use a separate mesh bag for each family member.

GOALS

- Discuss making a goal with your child. Choose a fun goal like learning to ride a skateboard. Then allow the child to write down everything that must be done to achieve the goal. Encourage your children to then make educational goals following the same format you would for other goals for themselves for the year.

- Post educational or family goals in special journals. Refer to them monthly or quarterly. This motivates students to achieve goals and provides accountability because the whole family knows about the goal. Encourage your child to do this with his friends as well.

- Encourage your child to post educational or family goals in special journals. Refer to them monthly or quarterly. This motivates students to achieve goals and provides accountability because the whole family knows about the goal. Encourage your child to do this with his friends as well.

- Tell your child to speak positively about himself. Remove the words "I can't" from your vocabulary.

HOME LIFE

- Assign a child to be Family Organizer for the week. This child can check to make certain the whole family is complying with the rules of order and organization. For instance, she might check to see if everyone is doing their chores. This is a great job for a middle child who often does not get the chance to take the lead or be influential in family decisions. Many families will acquiesce to the family baby or listen to a bossy oldest but this provides an opportunity for a middle child to shine.

- Encourage children to maintain an orderly room and desk at home by playing an occasional game of who can be the first to find the reading book (or some other object) from their desks or rooms in a specified amount of time. Thus children connect organizing to better management of their time.

- Teach your child proper telephone etiquette, including how to take an appropriate message correctly.

LEISURE TIME

- Put time in your schedule to play with your child. Allow the child to set the agenda. You will have more success when you want your child to cooperate with you. This also builds your relationship with your child.

- Designate a "kid zone." Set up a small corner in the family room just for your kids. This allows you to hang out together while they play and provides a set place for their stuff—which relieves you of having to cart it all back to their rooms each night. Make space for playthings. Toy baskets are a must in the living room and any other place your family spends time together. That way your children can have their stuff handy, and you can toss it all in the basket when you're expecting company.

- Limit television time. Have a start and finish time. You can purchase television and electronic game timers with tokens that your child must earn before he watches television or plays a game. The token system removes you from the position of regulating the time on the game system or television.

SCHOOLWORK

- Encourage your middle/high-school children (ages 10–18) to write out different facets of their school lessons, including introduction, closing and homework. This will later help them concentrate because they will be able to see how the lesson is segmented and how they can direct their attention to different aspects of the lesson.

- Ask your teen early, before a semester begins, to set goals for the school year including what grades he wants to get. You are teaching him that he is the master of his destiny; the destiny is not because of a bad teacher, ill scheduled class, lousy textbook, etc. If he decides he will achieve then once he is wired for success he will be successful.

- Put a start time and end time on homework sheets so your elementary age children (5–10 years) and middle-school youngsters (10–14 years) can monitor their time themselves. This will encourage them to concentrate on staying on task.

- Consider placing a bulletin board in your child's room. Your local hardware store sells wallboard that might not look too pretty and isn't framed, but a 4'x3' section is inexpensive and perfect for posting pertinent school items. You might want to paint it or cover it with burlap to improve its appearance or let your child take on this project.

- Keep organized notebooks. Help your child keep track of papers by organizing them in a binder or notebook. This will help him review the material for each day's classes and to organize the material later to prepare for tests and quizzes.

- Use dividers to separate class notes, or color-code notebooks. Separate "to do" and "done" folders help organize worksheets, notices, and items to be signed by parents, as well as providing a central place to store completed assignments.

- Conduct a weekly clean-up. Encourage your child to sort through book bags and notebooks on a weekly basis. Old tests and papers should be organized and kept in a separate file at home.

- Get your child a homework folder so he can place all completed homework in the folder. Some students lose their homework in the black hole of their backpacks.

- Get soft pencil grips for your child. Put them on all her pencils both at home and in school. It will help with her handwriting.

- Your child should be encouraged to utilize assignment sheets, broken down by day and subject. He or his teachers can record assignments at the completion of each task.

- One of the simplest interventions for forgetful children or students is to have an extra set of textbooks at home to minimize the problem of not having the necessary homework materials.

- Instruct your child to listen intently. Tell her to lean forward and comfortably toward the edge of her seat. This encourages active listening and will help her to grasp concepts quickly.

- Plastic storage cubes and hanging file folders solve paperwork storage for an older child. Color-code hanging file folders by subject. Inside each folder, individual files hold work-in-progress, worksheets to be corrected and daily lessons.

- Use lightweight, sturdy records boxes to hold school materials. Hanging file folders fit these boxes nicely. The boxes stack neatly and are easy to handle. Sort by child, curriculum, subject or year. Labeling is easy with permanent markers.

- Stackable letter trays serve many functions on a homework/child's desk. Use them to sort papers to correct, correspondence, or lesson plans.

- Color-code, color-code, color-code. Use color in hanging file folders, file folders, pens and labels. Whether it's child by child, subject by subject or unit by unit, color does the job!

- Give your child a checklist to review before he leaves for school. You should write the checklist in red or black ink and paste it to his notebook.

- Explain to your child how to keep his desk neat at school. Tell him to put all the big books on the bottom and little books on the top. Give him folders for loose papers.

- When you cover your child's textbooks for school, make certain to put the title clearly on the front and the spine of the book. It will be quicker and easier for her to locate an assigned book.

- Ask your child what she wants to be when she grows up. Then show her how developing good habits will help her reach her future goals (i.e. doing her math homework assignments will help her to become the architect she wants to be).

- Make certain your child's school bags have compartments. Decide together what each compartment will be used for. If you cannot find such a bag, then make your own by using small cosmetic/travel bags.

- Work with your child to associate the school dismissal bell ringing with immediately gathering all her supplies. Post a reminder note in her notebook or on her desk.

- Get your child graded workbooks to review schoolwork on summer and seasonal vacations.

- Encourage your child to breathe deeply and gather thoughts rather than just jumping in to answer questions on an exam.

- Teach your child to set a deadline before the teacher's deadline. In that way she can hand the project in and make changes if necessary.

- Encourage your child to learn relaxation techniques before an exam: tell her to breathe deeply and picture herself doing well on the exam.

- Tell your child to put his studying time in his calendar. Treat these times like appointments that must be kept.

- Help your child to look at her assignments and estimate how much time it will take her to complete them.

- Encourage your child to study in an uncluttered environment. An organized environment helps your child think more clearly.

TASKS

- Gently, not punitively, redirect your child when he is off a task. Often he doesn't realize it. It is not disobedience; it is merely a result of him being distracted. Gently give him nonverbal cues such as pointing or gently prodding him back to the task he was assigned.

- Reward your child when he can do a task with minimal verbal or tactile reminders.

- As much as possible attempt to give instructions in a quiet environment. Do not say "I already told you that" because most likely he did not hear you; simply repeat it in your normal voice tone.

- Praise your child for his little steps of success. He is probably feeling like a failure because he cannot complete a big task. Break down all big tasks into smaller tasks and reward your child for those little steps.

- Look your child in the eye and give verbal and physical (i.e. hugs) praise and affirmation when he has completed a task.

- Do not lecture kids when they fail to perform a task. Just state the agreement you all have decided to maintain as a family. A signed family contract and/or family constitution will help you implement this tip.

TIME MANAGEMENT

- Post dates to refresh class supplies (such as pencils, pens, crayons, etc.) on the family calendar and in your child's planner/organizer. Put the calendar in the time management center.

- Rotate the responsibility of family time and organization manager among siblings or between you and your child weekly. The family time manager gets to post things on the family calendar and to remind the family of appointments. We learn best by doing and giving your child the responsibility to actually monitor his time as well as the family's will do wonders for his self-esteem.

- Post calendars in kids' rooms, especially early elementary children with little concept of time. They can cross off the days until a special event occurs. You can also have them make the calendars themselves each month. Get blank calendars from websites or make them yourself.

- Insist your child has a schedule that he gives to you so that he can be accountable for keeping to the schedule. The schedule should also be posted in his planner or personal digital assistant.

- Use a flow chart so your teenager can visually mark his progress in a task. He can use index cards or post-it notes that he posts on the wall to get a clear idea of what he has to do and the time allotted to complete each task.

- ADD children can take very memorable notes when using graphic organizers. See our list of useful resources.

- Break down school projects and home tasks into small easy portions with estimated time to complete each activity or chore near the task. Some children are simply overwhelmed and do not realize time is simply passing them by when they are a bit distracted.

- Use a kitchen timer to establish the specific amount of time a child should be on task during independent work. Give children small intervals of time to complete work; then allow them to take a break. This will encourage children to stay on task because they can visually see an end to the task.

- Make a schedule for your child, because she really needs a lot of structure and even middle schoolers (ages 10–14) probably don't know how to make a realistic schedule because children tend to think idealistically.

- Put organizing time in your child's planner so that he understands that it is something he must do daily both in school and at home. Cite specific things he should do and provide visual cues.

- Post planning time in a schedule you make for your child. For instance, on completing homework, there should be a planned time of readying all materials for school the next day.

- Instruct your child to stop daydreaming by putting a dot on a piece of paper each time he catches himself daydreaming. After a while, he will be able to set a goal to track fewer dots. Reward him when you notice fewer dots.

- Schedule time in your child's day for a bit of daydreaming. This may go against what you have been told but if you constantly badger your child always to pay attention and be on task he has nothing to look forward to.

- Pair free time to task completion and remember to time this play or free time so that the child does not spend too much time idly. Einstein, who was said to have had a learning disability, felt imagination was more important than anything else.

- Any opportunity to practice time estimation is very helpful toward increasing such time awareness. For example, challenge your child to estimate how long it takes to walk to the bank or mailbox (without running), or any other task.

- Make a game out of predicting, timing and checking your child's time estimates for various activities.

- Monitor the assignment calendars, particularly monthly calendars of ADHD students. They tend to write things on the wrong date.

- Walk through the schedule each day and point out any changes in the daily/weekly schedule or routine that will be taking place.

- It is almost too obvious, but as soon as children can tell the time, they should have their own watch.

- Encourage your child to be honest about her shortcomings as related to time management. You will have to have an open mind yourself. People often procrastinate due to perfectionism, anger, etc.

- Post dial-a-teacher/tutor programs in your time management/homework station. Most school districts have a dial-a-teacher program. America Online (AoL) and other Internet providers have similar programs. High-school students can review concepts from middle school by calling these hotlines.

- Review your child's planner/organizer each week. Discuss ways she can improve her productivity. Brainstorm together.

- Teach your child to break down school projects and home tasks into small easy portions.

Useful Resources

EQUIPMENT

Alarm clocks

Extremely loud, flying, vibrating and moving alarm clocks are available from Sonic Boom, Princess International. A loud vibrating or moving alarm clock will stir even the heaviest sleeper. Of course, going to bed earlier should first be worked on but many parents report that their children respond well to these nontraditional alarm clocks.

TV/game time management system

These systems help you regulate your child's game usage and television consumption. Tokens are given that enable television or game usage for a specified time. You can tie the game time to homework or reading time.

Ear plugs

The ear plugs help your child to concentrate on homework or other tasks even in loud environments. You can get many different kinds. Do not let children, especially siblings, share ear plugs. 3M makes corded ear plugs that ensure your child will not lose them.

Noise machines

Some children actually can concentrate better with white noise. It also helps a very active child settle down and go to sleep. Sonic Boom makes an excellent and economical noise machine.

Electronic dictionary

This helps your children correct errors in spelling and vocabulary right away, which is especially useful if it would distract them to stop doing homework to look up a word. Franklin makes two spellers: one for elementary children (ages 5–10) and the other for middle school and high school (ages 10–18).

Electronic planner/PDA

Look at Palm's Tungsten line for the latest PDA. Your child should always use a paper planner with a digital back-up. ADHD children need the strong visual reminder that a paper calendar provides, especially if you color code dates and assignments.

Analog visual timer

Your child needs to see a visual presentation of time elapsing. Time Timer makes a visual timer that is also audible. In addition, timers need to be visually appealing. Young children will benefit from illuminated timers. There are many child-friendly timers on the market. Make sure the timer is durable by purchasing one from a reliable company.

Locker organizers/shelves

Lockers are notoriously messy if they do not have shelves or organizing magnets, etc. Locker organizing should occur at the beginning of the year and you should instruct your child to bring home all papers every Friday.

Classical/baroque music

It is proven that classical baroque music helps us concentrate. Many CDs are available. The traditional Masters' series is probably the best. You can get the CDs from anywhere, even your local library.

Suggested school supplies for homework center

Indelible black marker

Highlighters in several colors—especially yellow

Zip lock and sandwich bags—all sizes

Protractors

Compass

Rulers—in inches and centimetres

Glue and glue sticks

Spray adhesive

Scotch tape—wide and thin

Duct tape and packing tape

Fun or sticky tack

Thumb tacks

Paper clips—assorted sizes

Paper fasteners

Index cards—sizes 5x8" and 3x5", assorted colors

Notebook paper, wide and college ruled

Notebooks—spiral and composition notebooks

Graph paper and graph paper notebook

Card stock in white and colors

Lots of pencils—different colors, number two

Erasers—soft with no markings

Pens—red, blue and black ink

Markers—wide tip and fine point

Permanent magic markers—assorted colors

Computer paper—white and colored

Incentive stickers

Labels

Old magazines for assignments

Pencil cases

Notebook dividers

Looseleaf binders in several sizes

Sheet protectors

Tempera paint

Globe

Wall map

Atlas

Extra backpack

Set of encyclopedias or electronic encyclopedia

Dictionary—electronic and large comprehensive dictionary

Thesaurus—electronic and large comprehensive thesaurus

Calculators

Construction paper

White drawing paper

Folders—pocket and prong

Manila file folders

Envelopes

ADD/ADHD ORGANIZATIONS

United States

CHADD (Children and Adults with Attention Deficit/Hyperactivity Disorder)

www.chadd.org

CHADD is a national nonprofit organization providing education, advocacy and support for individuals with ADHD. In addition to informative information on their website, CHADD also publishes a variety of printed materials to keep members and professionals current on research advances, medications and treatments affecting individuals with ADHD.

Attention Deficient Disorder Association (ADDA)

www.add.org

The Attention Deficit Disorder Association (ADDA) is an organization that provides information, resources and networking to adults with ADD and to the professionals who work with them.

Attention Deficit Disorder Resources

www.addresources.org

This organization is dedicated to supporting, educating and serving as a resource for people with ADD.

UK

ADD/ADHD Online Information

www. adders.org

This website is quite exhaustive. It lists support groups in England, Scotland, Wales and Northern Ireland. It promotes awareness of ADD and provides a great deal of practical help.

Adult Attention Deficit Disorder

www.add.org
This organization provides assistance via local support groups in the UK.

Hyperactive Children's Support Group

www.hacsg.org.uk
This group offers practical advice and support to parents.

1 ADHD

www.4-adhd.com/adhd-directory/categories/online-support-groups.asp
This website will connect you to other websites that offer help, encouragement and services for ADD children and teenagers.

ADHDNews.com

www.adhdnews.com/adhd-resources.html
This website lists many different ADD organizations and support groups.

Canada

CHADD Children and Adults with Attention Deficiet Disorder

www.chaddcanada.org
This organization helps support individuals and families affected by ADD. It has many support groups and chapters across Canada.

Australia

Every Day With ADHD

www.everydaywithadhd.com
Provides support group details for ADD groups in Australia and New Zealand.

ADD/ADHD Online Information
www.adders.org/ausmap.htm
This site lists ADD/ADHD support groups in Australia.

Learning Difficulties Coalition
www.idc.org
This is a parental support group for children 5–18 years old. It offers assistance for parents whose children have ADD and other learning challenges.

International
ADDCoach4u
www.addcoach4u.com
This website offers coaching and has links to much more information as well as connecting the ADHD community

The Attention Deficit Hyperactivity Disorder Internet Links Project
www.attentiondeficitdisorder.ws
This website connects parents with ADD organizations worldwide.

BIBLIOGRAPHY
Carter, Cheryl R. (2009) *Clean Your Room So I Can At Least See the Floor.* Long Island, NY: Jehonadah Communications.
Carter, Jarret, Janae and Jolene (2002) *A Kid's Guide to Organizing.* Long Island, NY: Jehonadah Communications. This is a great book for your child to read. It is encourages your child to take steps to organize himself.
Kolberg, Judith and Nadeau, Kathleen (2002) *ADD Friendly Ways to Organize Your Life.* New York: Routledge.
Taylor, Blake E. S. (2008) *ADHD & Me: What I Learned from Lighting Fires at the Dinner Table.* Oakland, CA: New Harbinger. An interesting memoir written by an ADHD teenager.

Suggested Chores for Different Ages

2 YEARS TO 6 YEARS

Pick up their toys

Sort silverware

Put their clothes in labeled dresser drawers

Help sort laundry

Wipe down dinner/breakfast table

Wipe base boards

Pull up covers on their crib/toddler bed

Help load the dishwasher

Set the table

Weed the yard

Water plants

Use nontoxic spray cleaner in the bathroom and kitchen

Daily use disinfectant wipes in the bathroom

Empty wastebaskets

Use a handheld vacuum cleaner

Assist Mommy and Daddy with chores

7 YEARS TO 12 YEARS

The entire chore list for 2 years to 6 years and:

Wash and dry dishes

Rake leaves

Assist snow shoveling

Unload dishwasher

Damp mop floors

Vacuum floors

Make simple microwave meals

Wipe counters

Wipe down walls using nontoxic cleanser

Clean outdoor furniture

Assist in preparing family meals

Make their own beds

Clean their own rooms

Organize their toys

Take telephone messages

Do household filing

Assist in mowing the lawn

Dust furniture

Make shopping list

Put away groceries

Weed garden

Plant flowers in the yard

Wash siding

Make their own lunches

Wash the car

Help care for family pet

Sort mail

Organize family cassette tapes

Organize compact discs

Organize videocassette tapes

Clean windowsills

Water lawn

Take out garbage

13 YEARS TO 18 YEARS

The entire chore list for 7 years to 12 years and:

Prepare family meals

Go grocery shopping

Scrub the bathroom

Wax floors

Mow the lawn

Use the trimmer and cut hedges

Care for younger siblings

Clean the garage

Tutor siblings

Take care of family pet

Organize family files

Organize family library/books

Work as a secretary or receptionist in family home business

Wash blinds

Clean out refrigerator

Do their own laundry

Train younger siblings in household tasks

Polish furniture

Help plan the family budget

Chauffeur younger siblings to activities

Run errands for family

Example Checklists

AM CHECKLIST

Wake up

Turn off alarm clock

Pray

Bathroom time

Brush teeth

Wash face

Get dressed

Make bed

Breakfast

PM CHECKLIST

Tidy up bedroom

Put on pajamas

Brush teeth

Wash face

Pray

Read in bed

SCHOOL CHECKLIST
Night before

Pack lunch

Review your school schedule posted in school bag

Pack book bag and put near the door

Have parents sign all homework and notes, and give you trip money

Next morning

Pick up signed notes and items from parents

Double check your school bag

Check you have your lunch

Put on jacket/coat if needed

FUN FAMILY CHECKLIST

Did I hug everyone today?

Did I say an encouraging word today?

Did I help someone without being asked to do so?

Did I talk to God today?

Did I practice self-control today?

Did I play without bickering today?

Did I help Mom and Dad today?

Did I do my chores today?

Did I do my homework neatly today?

CLEAN ROOM CHECKLIST

Pick up all the toys and put away

Pick up all the papers and put away

Pick up all the clothes and put away

Pick up all the items that do not belong in the room

Sweep/vacuum floor

Chart and Planner Templates

DAILY TO-DO CHART SAMPLE

List activities and assign a value:

    A—Most important/must do!

    B—Should do/ought to do

    C—Could do/may do

A B or C	Time	Activity	Estimated time to complete
A	7.00	Finish Math homework	45 min

STUDY PLANNING SHEET SAMPLE

Project: Research paper on Thomas Jefferson

Preparation time	Resource	Estimated time	Other
Monday 4:15 pm	Library books	2 hours	Ask Dad to drive me to library
		Total time	

About the Author

Cheryl R. Carter is the founder of Organized Kidz, an organization that assists special needs children with organization and study skills. She is a former special needs teacher, organizing and time management consultant and freelance parenting writer who has worked with families for over 15 years. She is also a busy wife and mother who enjoys watching her children's soccer games, beating her husband at Scrabble and enjoying God in the ordinary. She is a former featured expert on LearningDisorders.com and also enjoys blogging. Visit www.add123.org for further information on ADD/ADHD.

Index